Moreton Morrell Site

D1355675

SHEAR GOLD

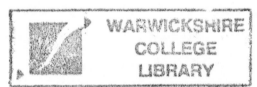

SHEAR GOLD

LESLIE LAW

With Gillian Newsum

Methuen

Published by Methuen 2005

10 9 8 7 6 5 4 3 2 1

Copyright © 2005 by Leslie Law and Gillian Newsum

The right of Leslie Law and Gillian Newsum to be identified as
authors of this work has been asserted by them in accordance with
the Copyright, Designs and Patents Act 1988

Methuen Publishing Ltd Reg. No. 3543167

A CIP catalogue record for this book
is available from the British Library

ISBN 0 413 77515 1

Typeset by SX Composing DTP, Rayleigh, Essex
Printed and bound in Great Britain by
St. Edmundsbury Press, Bury St. Edmunds, Suffolk

Contents

Acknowledgements

I would like to thank those people who have helped and encouraged me in writing this book, in particular Gillian Newsum for all her time and patience, and my mother, Margaret, for searching for many of those early pictures. My thanks also to John Beaton, whose initial idea it was, and to everyone at Methuen.

My gratitude goes to the team of people behind the scenes: my stable staff, farrier, vets, trainers, and especially my fiancée Trina Lightwood. Together they have made an enormous contribution to realising the dream of a gold medal in Athens.

A special thanks must go to all my owners for their invaluable support throughout my career, and also to the many sponsors that have provided much needed financial support over the years, including Shearwater Insurance.

Lastly, the biggest thank you is to the horses, without whom none of this would have been possible. I owe them everything.

I gratefully acknowledge the following for permission to use photographs: John Britter Photography, picture 16; Trevor Meeks (courtesy of *Horse and Hound*), pictures 18, 21, 27–32, 34, 37. All other pictures are from my family's collection.

Introduction

It was Yogi Breisner who broke the news to me. He had been the British team manager since the Sydney Olympics in 2000, and had become a friend and mentor. I had already been told that the decision by the Court of Arbitration for Sport was likely to be announced at around 3pm that day, but I couldn't sit at home and wait for it. Two of my horses were entered in the Novice class at Solihull horse trials, so I was committed to compete that day. I didn't want let down the owners and, besides, I thought the event would take my mind off the impending announcement.

My mobile phone rang as I was warming-up a horse called Diamond Hall Alice for the show jumping. It was Yogi. "You're not going to believe this," he said, "You've got the gold!" There was a long silence, then, "Hello. Leslie? Are you there?" I was speechless. It seemed unbelievable that after the confusion, drama and emotional snakes and ladders of the final day of the eventing at Athens, the individual gold medal was now mine. It was the first time a British rider had won an Olympic Gold in eventing since Richard Meade in 1972. I didn't know what to say or do. Then the phone rang again, and again. People were ringing to congratulate me. In the end I decided to switch it off and get on with my show jumping round, but my concentration, held in check for the best part of the day, was now shattered and, as if to remind me of my luck in Athens where Shear L'Eau had touched the planks but they had remained in place, Diamond Hall Alice ground to a standstill in front of the planks in the show jumping arena at Solihull. Even gold medallists make mistakes.

The owners of Diamond Hall Alice, and another novice horse, Best of Spirits, were very understanding and agreed with me that it wasn't going to be sensible to run them on the cross country. Solihull horse trials was already swarming with press who had heard that an announcement on the medals was imminent and the interest in me by now was overwhelming. Some of the non-equestrian reporters were aghast to find me competing at a novice event (or "gymkhana" as one local paper described it) within hours of returning from the Olympic Games in Athens, where I had initially been awarded individual silver and team bronze. But I had fifteen horses in the yard at home waiting to be worked and competed, so things had just carried on as usual.

If there hadn't been such a mix up with the scoring in Athens and I had been awarded the gold medal at the time, I think I would have stayed on to the end of the Games and returned with the other Olympic gold medallists to be part of the reception at Gatwick. It would have been amazing – the moment of a lifetime – to stand on the winner's podium in the equestrian stadium at Athens and be presented with my gold medal, to hear the national anthem and bask in a moment of glory . . . but I don't feel bitter about it.

In fact, at first I was delighted to get the silver: winning an individual medal had already exceeded my expectations. But with the knowledge that the German rider, Bettina Hoy, had made a mistake in her first show jumping round, going through the start twice, there came the realization that my silver medal should really have been a gold one, and it was an unsatisfactory end to the event. The FEI (International Equestrian Federation) appeal committee had ruled in Bettina's favour in Athens, and she was awarded the gold medal. But the committee had exceeded its authority and had been wrong to intervene in a dispute over rules. Three days later, when we were all back at home and life was beginning to return to normal, the Court of Arbitration for Sport overturned the appeal committee's decision, taking away Bettina's medal – a ghastly thing to happen to her – and awarding it to me. It was a strange way to win.

Has it changed my life? Yes, but not dramatically. I've always been a realistic person and never allowed myself to get on too much of a "high" when things have gone well, because the fall is even greater when it all goes wrong. It's a way of protecting myself, cushioning myself from the lows – and there have been enough of them. The problem with the sport of eventing is that there are two of you in the equation, horse and rider, so there are twice as many pitfalls; and the cross country test, which is central to the event, is full of risk and uncertainty. On any one day the rider might be fit and well, but the horse might be off-form, or vice versa. To win a big event, both rider and horse must be at their best for three days in a row. Luckily for me, this is exactly what we managed to achieve in Athens. Everything came right for me there, when it really mattered.

The most immediate effect of knowing that I had won the gold medal was a huge sense of relief. I had finally won a major event: that elusive first place was mine at last. Time and again I had just missed the top place (a second and third at Badminton, and fourth individual at the 2002 European Championships), and self-doubt had begun to creep in.

Whenever I went to a team championship, or to Badminton, Burghley or Lexington (the three main four-star events) I was becoming increasingly anxious to do well. There are more people to please in this sport than just oneself. The owners of the horses, your trainers, grooms and supporters also have expectations. The pressure was mounting for me to prove that I could win a major prize and pay back those people who had put their trust, money and hard work behind me. Then suddenly, after one call on my mobile phone, I was an Olympic champion.

I tend to keep out of the limelight. In fact, in the last five years there has probably been less written about me than any of the other three regular British team members (Pippa Funnell, William Fox-Pitt and Jeanette Brakewell). Even so, I can't say I didn't enjoy the attention that followed my gold medal announcement. The strangest request came from my local radio station, BBC Hereford and Worcester. They wanted me to donate a bag of Shear L'Eau's manure to be auctioned to raise money for a hospital charity. I didn't think anyone would pay much for it, but to my amazement it went for £760 on eBay!

One drawback of becoming the gold medallist was that, overnight, I was expected to become a spokesman for the sport. When anything happened, I was asked for a comment, and of course there was a lot of coverage about me at the start of Burghley, where I was competing with Shear H20, full brother of Shear L'Eau, two weeks after returning from Athens. On the first day, Lady Victoria Leatham, the daughter of Lord Burghley, let me pose with her father's gold medal from 1928 (440 yards hurdles), as my own gold medal was still on its way back from Germany, and on Sunday there was to be a parade for the Olympic team. It was all good fun, but late on Saturday afternoon things went horribly wrong. Caroline Pratt was killed in a horrendous fall on the cross country and Burghley was plunged into gloom.

The tragedy left everyone involved feeling utterly devastated, and it put the sport back in the spotlight, this time for the wrong reason. On Sunday morning there was a major press conference about the accident, and I was asked to speak: something I was not at all keen to do. Coming to terms with Caroline's death was bad enough – she had been a friend as well as a fellow member of the British squad – let alone facing the press. In the end Yogi persuaded me to do it and it didn't go too badly, but there weren't any more gold medal celebrations after that. I had been well and truly brought back down to earth, and even my subsequent fifth place at Burghley gave me little pleasure. It's a good thing I'm a realist.

1
Early Days

I never dreamt of becoming an Olympic champion when I was a boy
messing about on ponies with Willy Bryan, my best friend and
accomplice on many childhood adventures. At that time it never
occurred to me that such a thing would be possible, or even
desirable. I had no contact with the sort of people who were
competing at a high level in the sport, and I had never been to a
three-day event, so I didn't even have much idea of what the sport
was all about. I don't think I was a dreamer anyway. Life was more
immediate. Would we win the next school football match? When
could we go to Willy's place to ride again? Would Mum and Dad
buy us a pony? Could they afford it?

For a young boy with too much energy, I couldn't have asked for
a better childhood. We didn't have a lot of money, but we did have
freedom. I could take off on a bike whenever I liked, or go for long
walks with my younger brother Graham. We would mess about in
streams, climb trees, throw sticks at each other, play football in the
village street with the other boys – just about anything we wanted.
In the school holidays we'd be out from morning until dark, coming
home only when we were hungry.

We were lucky because we lived in a very rural part of England: a
village called Bredwardine in Herefordshire. My father, Lawson, had
been a lorry driver for a mobile home company in Hereford, but
when the company gave up the transport side of the business, Dad
bought the huge transporter lorry from them and set up on his own.
We were living in a terraced council house with a tiny garden, so he

had to rent a yard nearby to park the lorry, and from there he started dealing in second-hand mobile homes and caravans. He was very enterprising, always looking out for things that he could make money on. He used to buy tatty old caravans at auctions, bring them back to the yard, and Mum would clean and spruce them up, before advertising them in the Hereford Times.

I met Willy Bryan at the local primary school in Kinersely. There were no more than 24 children at the school, and Willy was in my year. His father, Bill, is a great horseman: what you'd call an old-fashioned nags man. There isn't much he doesn't know about horses, and he has an incredible way with them. He's had hundreds of point-to-point winners and has won countless show classes at Wembley. Graham and I used to go back to his yard after school and play on the ponies. I wasn't particularly good at riding them, but could just about stay on. It was Graham who was the keen one; he got very interested and persuaded our parents to let him have his own pony.

I was about ten years old then and Graham was eight. I think my father must have worked all hours to get enough money. I remember we went off to Abergavenny market to look for a pony, and came back with two – one for each of us. We rented a field, and after a few weeks of bareback riding we managed to get hold of some saddles. My little mare was called Grey Lace. She could be quite wicked, and frequently ejected me, very easily, by dropping her shoulder. We had a lot of fun, but we fell off more times than we stayed on so eventually my mother decided it would be sensible for us to have some lessons. A local lady called Charmaine Turner gave us our first lessons. We learnt how to hold the reins properly and do rising trot, which was a significant step forward.

We probably weren't the easiest of children to teach: typical small boys, I suppose. As soon as we could trot we wanted to canter, and as soon as we could canter we wanted to gallop. We'd meet up with Willy sometimes and go off for long rides, mostly at the gallop. About two years later Mum and Dad bought their own house in Eardisley, a bigger village than Bredwardine, but nearby. We still didn't have any land for the ponies, and had to rent a field three miles away, but we did have a garage, which we used as a stable, so at least the ponies could be on site some of the time. The garage had an up-and-over door, so it had to be left up, and we fixed a bar across the entrance.

Another advantage of moving to Eardisley was that there was a family living near us called the Preeces, who had a farm in the village. Their two children, Daphne and Elizabeth, were keen riders, and they introduced us to the local Pony Club, the Golden Valley, and we started going to rallies. They also encouraged us to go hunting, which we both loved, and we would often be "sick" on a Friday so that we could miss school to go hunting.

By now I was at the Lady Hawkins comprehensive in Kington, but I was beginning to lose interest in school. I found that the more riding I did, the more I realised I just wanted to work with horses. The only stimulating thing at school was the football – Willy and I were both on the school soccer team, which we loved. My parents thought the riding thing was just a passing fad, but they were always very encouraging. Neither of them had any experience with horses, but they were very happy to take us to all the Pony Club activities. They got very involved, and gave us all the support they could. They would watch us compete, or take us hunting and follow around in the car all day until we'd finished.

Our Pony Club days were brilliant. The club was run by a great hunting family: Hazel Bishop was our district commissioner, and her husband, Vivien, was the Master and huntsman of the Golden Valley Foxhounds. Willy, Graham and I were among only a handful of boys in the Pony Club, which was good fun, especially at camp; and I got onto the Pony Club teams, which also increased my enthusiasm.

My parents had a strong influence on me. Whatever my father does, he always strives to do it to the best of his ability, and I think this has brought out the competitor in me. My mother, Margaret, was very strict with us – she probably needed to be – so she instilled the discipline, which I still have, though it has been known to lapse a bit sometimes. Dad, being Dad, couldn't resist dealing in horses, just as he did in caravans. If he was passing Abergavenny on a

Saturday, there was always a chance that he'd call in at the sales and come home with some unbroken three-year-old.

So having spent only about two years learning to ride, we found ourselves breaking in ponies and taking them to hunter trials and Pony Club events, and then if they went well Dad would sell them on for a good profit. I remember we had a roan pony that we named Little George after Chicken George in *Roots*, which we had been watching on TV at the time. Dad had bought him for about thirty guineas and we sold him two years later for over six hundred. It was a bit tough on us sometimes, but it made us learn how the wheels go round in life.

When I was fourteen I got my first really good pony. He was called Barry and we bought him in Malvern. I remember he was quite expensive, but he was lovely: he could move and he looked the part, so we could actually attempt dressage! I did the Pony Club area teams with him, but he soon got sold on as well, and we started looking for a horse. We found a wild, three-year-old chestnut mare in Hereford market that had just been broken in, and we called her Little Clearway because she was sired by a horse called Clear Run. The only chance we had of staying on her was to ride her on the end of a lunge line in one of the Preeces' ploughed fields. She was so sharp, and she could buck for England! We used to try to wear her out in the heavy plough, where if you fell off at least it didn't hurt too much. We had certainly taken on more than we were ready for with Little Clearway, but in the end she turned out to be a fabulous horse, and Graham rode her on the Junior Event team at the European championships at Rotherfield Park in 1985.

Although Little Clearway and others were giving me an interesting equine education, along with some strong lessons in character building, I can't say I was doing quite so well at school. I had already decided that I was going to work with horses, so I couldn't see any point in worrying about exams. Dad wasn't too concerned, because he'd made his own way in life through hard work rather than relying on qualifications, but Mum was more aware of the need for a decent education. She was the one who did the books at home; she was good with figures and she kept our feet firmly on the ground, so she was probably a bit disappointed with my GCSE results. I passed Maths, Physics and two English exams. As soon as I left school I went to work at Bill Bryan's yard.

It was a great experience working there, as well as good fun. Willy and I were riding up to ten horses a day: point-to-pointers, show horses, hunters, youngsters, all sorts. We got plenty of good advice from Bill (and plenty of bollockings as well), and learnt a lot by watching him, but we also learnt a huge amount by trial and error. You soon discovered that the first time you went into a stable with one of the unbroken youngsters that were sent to Bill's yard straight off a mountain in Wales, you needed to shut the top door or you'd lose him. Then once you'd managed to get a roller on him, you'd get out of the stable mighty quick because, as you'd also discovered, the horse was going to hit the roof.

Willy and I enjoyed exercising the hunt liveries. We were supposed to take them down the road for a quiet hack, but we were often tempted to have a bit of fun. We would jump a hedge off the road, whip across the fields, jump a couple more hedges and then jump back onto the road. We used to dare each other: "I bet you can't jump that hedge onto the road and then go straight across and jump the next hedge into the other field." So of course you had to do it. We used to hunt a lot as well. Bill was a great hunting man and we'd go along with him. He'd usually have a few drinks along the way, so we'd end up bringing him home at the end of the day – sometimes having to drive the lorry for him, even though neither of us had a license.

We got away with our antics most of the time, though I do remember getting into serious trouble one day because we'd got Willy's younger brother completely soaked while out on a hack. That part of Herefordshire, near Letton, was particularly prone to flooding, and Willy and I had been enjoying galloping the horses through the floodwater in the fields. In the middle of one of these fields was a brook, which you couldn't see because of the floodwater, but we knew it was there and the horses had got used to fumbling their way down into it and up the other side. That day we took Willy's brother out with us on his 12.2 hands pony and we started racing through the water across this field, shouting, "Come on, Simon, gallop through the water!" We knew what was coming, but he didn't, and when he got to the brook his pony galloped straight in and disappeared! We did start to panic a bit then, but the two of them soon emerged – drenched from head to toe.

The point-to-points were always a great social time, and Bill was very successful with his horses. Willy's older brother Johnny was a good amateur jockey and he rode most of the racehorses. I rode in a few point-to-points, but I wasn't particularly good. I was still competing with Little Clearway, doing some Pony Club events and show jumping, and I did my first BHS (now BE) affiliated event on her at Crookham. In spite of the lessons I'd been having with David Pincus, a good instructor who had recently moved to Herefordshire, and the help I'd had from Daphne Preece, we came about fourth last in the dressage at Crookham. But Little Clearway was nippy, and we went clear cross country and clear in the show jumping to win our novice section. Nowadays you wouldn't have a hope of winning a section from such a poor dressage place.

Another of Dad's Abergavenny purchases turned out to be a very good working hunter pony. He'd bought the pony, which we called Little Boy Blue, as a two-year-old, and we turned it out in the field for a year. He grew to about 14.2 hands, and when we got him back up, broke him in, pulled his mane and tidied him up we found we had a rather beautiful pony. As a four-year-old he qualified for the fifteen hands novice working hunter at the Peterborough BSPS championships. We had no idea what the championships would be like, but as we'd qualified, we thought we should go.

The place was full of small girls in pig-tails and ribbons, with roses pinned to immaculate navy jackets; there were coloured brow-bands on the ponies, smart showing crops – you name it, they had it. There were about 48 ponies in our class, but only seven got round the jumps. The rest were eliminated, and we were one of only two clears. We went back in for the judging and won the class, so then we had to stay on for the next day to go into the championship. The organisers found us a spare stable and we slept in the trailer, but it was worth the effort because we were reserve champion in the end.

When we came home from Peterborough, even I agreed that this was the moment to sell the pony. We weren't really into showing, and I was already a bit big for him, so I rang up a local pony judge who had told us that he thought the pony would make a good working hunter. He suggested I contact Andy Croft, who bought horses for clients in the showing world (he and his wife Jane also owned one of Pippa Funnell's horses), but I didn't have a clue who he was. I told him I wanted £4,000 for the pony, which was a lot of money twenty years ago. When he told me he took a ten per cent commission, I said I still wanted £4,000, so he'd have to get his commission on top of that! He must have wondered who this jumped-up little twerp was, but he came back to me a few days later with a potential client. It was Lisa Hale. That was my first introduction to the Hales, and I've stayed in touch with them and ridden horses for them on and off ever since. I currently have a talented horse of theirs called Kif d'Estruval, which they originally bought for racing, but he wasn't quite quick enough so he is now eventing. Lisa also did some eventing after her showing career, and then moved into show jumping. She and her father own Nick Skelton's top horse, Arko.

While I was still based with the Bryans, we used to show jump quite regularly during the winter at an indoor arena on the other side of Hereford. We'd go there at the weekends, or sometimes in the evenings. This is where I met Ian Silitch, an American rider, who had set up in partnership with Revel Guest, joint master of the Golden Valley Foxhounds. Ian had come over to England to stay with the Guests, who were friends of his family, and he and Revel had decided to set up a business buying young horses in England and selling them in America. The idea was to jump the horses over here during the winter, take them back to America in the spring to do a bit more jumping, and then sell them on.

Ian, who was 25 years old at the time, had seen me at the arena and offered to help me with my jumping. I didn't actually think I needed any help, as I was already winning classes, but that just highlighted the difference between the British and American mentality, and the way we went about our riding. The American way is all about tuition, and Ian was already teaching in America. We got talking, and Ian asked me if I'd like to go and work for him in America, as a working pupil. It sounded like a good idea to me.

2
Taking Off

Going out to America at the age of eighteen was quite an eye-opener. I hadn't travelled much in England, let alone abroad, and I hadn't been to any big international shows or events in England. So to be working on the American show jumping circuit, seeing all the top riders like Joe Fargis, Leslie Burr and Katie Monaghan, was fantastic. I went from sleeping in my own room at home in Eardisley, to staying in hotels and motels (often sleeping on the floor, admittedly) all over the east coast of America.

It was in the heyday of American show jumping. The legendary George Morris was training their team riders, and I was out there for the Los Angeles Olympics when the US team got the gold medal and Joe Fargis won the individual gold. To be around at that time, and to watch these riders in action, was a great experience. Horses were changing hands for tens of thousands of US dollars – and I thought I'd done well when I sold Little Boy Blue for £4,000. It made me feel as if I had only been fooling around with horses at Bill's yard. The Americans were very professional in their approach to their riding and they did a lot of training. In England it had been much more hit and miss, particularly for me, and I certainly hadn't learnt about looking for a stride to a fence. I just used to kick on and hope for the best.

I spent two years working for Ian, based first in Vermont and later in Virginia, and learnt a huge amount about producing horses for show jumping; and I think I grew up a bit too. It did me good to have to fend for myself and to take on more responsibility. We had a lot of fun as well. There was another lad working for Ian full time called Phillip, and a lot more people turned up at the weekends, mostly teenagers who kept horses or ponies at Ian's barn and had lessons with him. They would compete in shows at the weekends, and we would look after their horses during the week, so it was always a lively environment.

The only drawback was that I didn't have an American work permit, so I had to go home every six months, get another six-month visa, and come back again. This ploy was successful for about eighteen months, then on one trip back to the States I was stopped by Immigration Control and given a serious gruelling. They went through my suitcase and wallet and asked me a lot of questions. Where was I going? Who was I staying with? You're coming here to work aren't you? I kept saying "no" to the last question, but they went on and on at me, for hours. I kept insisting that I was just a tourist, but I was very worried. I had a horrible feeling I'd be catching the next plane back to England.

In the end they just stamped my passport for another six months and let me go, but after that I decided I wouldn't chance my luck again. The next time I came back to England I stayed. I continued to work for Ian and Revel, based at Revel's yard at Cabalva House near Hay-on-Wye. It was around this time that I came up with the bright idea of channelling those horses that were not going to make the grade as show jumpers into eventing. The plan was for me to put a bit of form on these horses, and then we'd sell them on, either in England or to Americans. So gradually more of my time was spent bringing on event horses.

Being based at Cabalva was also an eye-opener, but for different reasons. The Guests were a well-established local family. Raymond Guest, a first cousin to Revel, owned racehorses like L'Escargot, winner of the Cheltenham Gold Cup and the Grand National, and Sir Ivor, who won the Derby. Raymond was like a father to Revel, and he gave her away at her wedding when she married an American lawyer called Rob Albert. Revel was a joint-master of the Golden Valley Foxhounds and also a successful businesswoman: she ran a company called Transatlantic Films, which made documentaries.

She and Rob would spend the week in London and then come back to Cabalva at weekends, often bringing friends with them. Their guests were mostly high-flying, professional people, who used to terrify me.

It was a very different scene from America, where I had felt well within my safety zone in the company of Ian, Philip and their friends. At Cabalva, weekends were all about entertaining, dinner parties and so on, and I was expected to join in. This was something I had never done. Revel was adamant that I should come to the dinner parties: these people could be potential buyers for her horses! Many visitors were based in London, so it was wonderful for them to come to Herefordshire for the weekend to stay at Cabalva, a lovely big house that backed onto the River Wye with views over to the Black Mountains. I suppose Revel thought that if they enjoyed themselves in the country, they might just want to buy an event horse, which I could ride for them. So it was my job to tell them all about the sport, a job I found painfully difficult to do.

Most of the time I was completely out of my depth. I was twenty years old, I had four GCSEs to my name, and I'd spent most of my short life riding horses. To be expected to mingle with these people and talk to them at dinner parties, when the conversation was usually well over my head, was agony. In the end, I told Revel how much I hated it, and said that, if it was all right with her, I'd rather spend Saturday nights at the pub with my mates. I didn't get a very good response. She explained that the horses were a business that had to pay, that we had to make it work, and talking to these people was part of the job. I didn't appreciate it at the time, but her insistence that I learnt to cope with these dinner parties was worth a bucketful of GCSEs.

Revel was brilliant. She made me appreciate my own worth by explaining that her guests might well be clever lawyers or businessmen, but they didn't know anything about horses and riding; or if they did, they certainly hadn't got the knowledge or ability I had. She made me sit next to her at dinner and would help instigate conversations about horses to get me going. With her to guide me, I was able to gain in confidence, to talk more and to pick up information. I also listened to Revel talking to people and watched how she would persuade them to get involved in her documentaries. She could even tempt someone who wasn't horsey to take an interest in eventing and perhaps buy a horse, or at least a share in one.

This was the best education I had ever had. Coming from a background where I didn't have any "connections" with wealthy people, learning to talk to them with reasonable confidence was very important if I wanted to survive in the sport. I was never going to have enough money to buy and keep my own horses, so I would have to rely on other people wanting me to ride theirs. They certainly weren't going to ask me if I couldn't communicate with them. While based with Revel I also came into contact with leading show jumpers like Bill Steinkraus and Peter Robeson, who sometimes gave me lessons.

Within two years of starting to work for Revel at Cabalva I competed in my first Burghley. Looking back, that seems like an incredibly rapid breakthrough. I had only done a few affiliated one-day events on Little Clearway before going to work in America, so, unlike my younger brother Graham, I hadn't even got as far as being considered for junior or young rider teams. Graham had taken over the ride on Little Clearway when I went to the States, and did very well on her. In 1985 he came fifth in the National Junior Championships at Windsor and was subsequently selected for the British junior team at the European Championships at Rotherfield Park, where he finished seventh.

When I began working at Cabalva I was bringing on novice horses to be sold, so most of my competing was at novice level. I did have an Intermediate horse called Night Flight III that I had been asked to ride by some local friends, the Eckleys, because their son Mark was going away to college, but I hadn't come anyway near competing at Advanced level because we never kept a horse long enough for me to get that far. Fortunately, Revel was usually quite happy for me ride other people's horses – she would charge them for it, but that was all part of the business – and it was through Revel that I got my first chance to compete at the top level, on Sam Barr's stallion Welton Apollo.

Revel had sent one of her mares to the Welton Stud in Gloucestershire, and when she rang up to see how the mare was getting on, Sam happened to mention that Linda Huggins, his partner at the time, had flu so she couldn't ride Welton Apollo at Weston Park at the weekend. The next thing I knew, Revel had organised for me to ride the horse. I rushed down to the Welton Stud on the Thursday to have a sit on him, and then rode him in the Advanced Class at the weekend. We came seventh. After that, I kept the ride on him, which was a great boost for me as he had already had three other riders – Diana Clapham, Polly Schwerdt and Linda. I did four more Advanced classes on him that year (1986) and was placed in all of them, winning at Kings Somborne.

So then it was on to Burghley. I don't remember feeling particularly nervous about competing in my first four-star three-day event – perhaps it was a case of "ignorance is bliss". Ginny Leng (née Holgate, and now Elliot) walked the cross-country with me and gave me as much advice as she could about the event, which was a great help. Ginny was also riding some of the Welton horses at this time, so Sam Barr had arranged for me to go to Ivyleaze, the Holgate's home, for some help during the summer and I had lessons there with Dot Willis, Ginny's trainer.

Dot was a very strict teacher, and made me much more disciplined about my training. Each thing that I did with the horse had to be right before I could go on to the next. In spite of her help, my test at that first Burghley was really just a case of going through the motions. We were well down the field after the dressage, though we hadn't disgraced ourselves. Ginny went into the lead on Murphy Himself, who was only eight years old at the time, and went clear cross-country and show jumping to win the event from the American Bruce Davidson. It was her fourth successive win at Burghley. My performance was less impressive: I had a stop on the cross-country at a fence called The Weir, which had running water going through it. I think Welton Apollo decided he needed to take a closer look. We also had three fences down in the show jumping and finished up in 42nd place, which I suppose wasn't too bad for a first attempt. The last six months had been a very steep learning curve.

When I had first begun riding for Revel I hadn't even thought about competing at Badminton; that sort of thing seemed light years away, as we were busy buying young horses, producing them and selling them on. Now, suddenly, it was the next thing on the agenda. I had a successful pre-Badminton run at Weston Park in March (1987), where we came fourth, so things were looking promising until a deluge of rain reduced the Badminton estate to a quagmire and the event was cancelled. So much for my Badminton début.

I did at least have the consolation of winning one of the two-star sections at Windsor the following month with Night Flight – my first three-day event win – and I also continued to have a good season in the Advanced classes with Welton Apollo, so we set our sights on Burghley again. This time things did not go at all well. We did a slightly better dressage, but were eliminated at the fourth fence on the cross country, which was, embarrassingly, the fence in the main arena. Welton Apollo ran out three times at the rather awkward corner. This was my first serious failure with the horse, and I felt very disappointed. I think I had reached the top level of the sport so quickly (perhaps a little too quickly) because I was such a competitive rider. Clearly, there was still a lot for me to learn, though I'm not sure I appreciated that at the time. I certainly wasn't going to be put off having a go at Badminton the following spring.

The only time I had been to Badminton was in 1986 when Revel was making a film about the different horse sports. I had thought the cross-country course looked all right, but then I wasn't riding. Two years later it looked a whole lot different. Welton Apollo was only sixteen hands, and the jumps suddenly looked very big. I remember thinking, "Can he really get across these?" Once again, my dressage was a case of going through the motions, rather badly, and we were placed 41st out of the 56 starters. In those days though, it was never too late to make amends for a poor dressage score by going well in the cross-country, and even with one stop going into the Lake, due mostly I suspect to my lack of experience, we pulled up to eighteenth place. So all in all, it wasn't too bad for a first Badminton, though I obviously had a long way to go before I could emulate the likes of Ian Stark, who made history that year by finishing first and second on Sir Wattie and Glenburnie.

By now I was beginning to get some more good horses to ride. Through my contact with the Holgates, I competed a nice young stallion based with them called Espiritu, with whom I won the two-star event at Osberton in the autumn after my first Badminton ride. Espiritu, who was eventually sold to Canada, was by Master Spiritus, also the sire of Ginny's excellent horse Master Craftsman. The Holgates were tremendously supportive of me at this time, and gave me some of their novice horses to ride. One of them was Welton Chit-Chat, with whom I won the one-star event at Tweseldown, and who went on to win Bramham with Ginny in 1991 before being sold to the Spanish rider Santago Centenera. It was a great experience for me to be involved with the Holgates because, as a team, Dot, Heather and Ginny were the most professional outfit at the time – the original Spice Girls with lots of girl power!

The following year (1989) I had more success at Windsor, coming first in the Long Walk section on Park Hall, a horse owned by Bernice Cuthbert, and second in the Copper Horse section on Spaceman, an Irish-bred horse that Revel had bought. Both horses were later sold to Americans. Windsor seemed to be my lucky event in those days: the next year, I won two sections: one on a horse called Haig, owned by Mary Archdale, and the other on Cappamore, but I've never won at the event since then. Cappamore came to the yard when Juliet Sandford started working for Revel at Cabalva. She had bought him from Ireland as a four-year-old, but he didn't stop growing and she ended up with a horse that was nearly seventeen hands. He turned out to be too much for her, and she asked me to compete him. In the same way, Haig, also seventeen hands, was a bit too big for Mary Archdale.

In 1989 I came back for my second attempt at Badminton with Welton Apollo, and this time we had a more successful outing. Our dressage had improved significantly and we went into eleventh place at the end of the first two days, and followed that up with a great cross-country round. Welton Apollo was a very good horse to ride cross-country. One of the characteristics of a stallion is to be a little bit stuffy, so I always had to ride Welton Apollo very strongly at his fences, but I felt confident doing this because he was a super technician in front. He never left a leg on anything so I could keep riding him forward and, because he didn't pull, he was very fast. In fact, if I didn't keep riding him positively all the time I risked having a stop, even on an Intermediate course.

He certainly taught me to ride forward, but it was a way of riding that I enjoyed. Having been in America where they tend to ride in a very forward style in the show jumping, my cross-country riding was an adaptation of that style, but in a higher gear. Because of that, I think Welton Apollo suited me and I suppose I suited him. We just seemed to click. Our clear cross-country round at Badminton, with only four time penalties, brought us up to sixth place, but two fences down in the show jumping the next day dropped us back down to eighth. It was good enough, though, for us to be selected to compete at the European Championships in the autumn.

The championships were held at Burghley that year, and because Britain was hosting the event we were allowed to have twelve riders competing: four on the team and eight individuals. Not surprisingly, I was selected to ride as an individual. We had a very experienced team with Ginny Leng (Master Craftsman), Ian Stark (Glenburnie) and Lorna Clarke (Fearliath Mor). The only newcomer to the team was Rodney Powell (The Irishman), who must be one of the most unlucky event riders I know. Before making his debut at Burghley, Rodney had been short listed for the British team six times, but for one reason or another had always missed out at the last moment. When he did finally ride for a senior team, he went brilliantly on the cross-country to go into second place at the end of the day, only to suffer a huge disappointment when The Irishman was rejected at the final horse inspection.

Mark Phillips had designed the cross-country course at Burghley, and it was certainly a tough one, but that probably worked in favour of the home side. British riders swept the board. All our team riders completed the cross-country clear within the optimum time, and we won the team gold medal with 145 penalties to spare from Holland, while Ginny Leng collected her third consecutive European title with three show jumps in hand. Jane Thelwall took the individual silver and Lorna Clarke the bronze. I was definitely an "also ran" on that occasion, as a result of a fall at the Trout Hatchery. We had to jump over a curved wall into the Upper Trout Hatchery and then go through the water and up a step onto a bank (which was under a roof) and then jump back into the Lower Trout Hatchery. Welton Apollo tripped up the step onto the bank and I fell off, so that was that. It wasn't quite the performance I had been hoping for at my first international championship, but at least we completed the event.

3

For Better or for Worse

During the 1989 season I met Harriet Harrison, a granddaughter of Rex Harrison. She was a keen event rider and we had seen each other at various competitions, so in the winter I made an excuse to see her again by inviting her to Cabalva to go hunting. Harriet was a very outgoing, bubbly person and I think I found her particularly exciting and intriguing because she came from such a different background to me. They say opposites attract, and I think that was certainly the case for us. Harriet had been brought up in America among film stars, musicians and theatre people – a very different and rather more flamboyant lifestyle than mine. When her parents split up, she came to live in England with her mother, who later married David Salmon. I think there had been a lot of changes in her life, whereas mine had always been very solid and stable, with strong family ties, and perhaps it was that sense of security that attracted Harriet to me. My life had been quite sheltered and, in spite of what I had learnt through working for Revel Guest, I wasn't very aware of what went on in the world. Harriet was the opposite: open-minded and prepared to take risks. Ironically, those things that had so attracted us to each other eventually drove us apart.

Harriet moved in with me at the yard at Cabalva at the beginning of the 1990 season, bringing her horses with her. It couldn't have been better for me because not only did I have this wonderful girlfriend living with me, but she was also very good at dressage and could help me with my flatwork. The season started well with a win for me in an Intermediate section at Crookham on Welton Apollo, and high placings with him at Ston Easton, Belton Park and Kings Somborne. At Badminton, though, we had an annoying stop on the cross-country and finished well down the line in 24th place, which was disappointing after my success there the previous year. At least I was getting some good results with other horses at the yard: Haig, a big, free-moving horse owned by Mary Archdale, and Cappamore, also a large horse, each won a section at Windsor three-day event, and I came third at Bramham on Treasure Island, an Advanced level horse that Revel had bought from Chris and Anne Hooley in Herefordshire. In the summer I took Welton Apollo to Gatcombe for the British Open Championships and was delighted when we finished fourth, as this was his last event before retiring. He then returned to Sam Barr's yard to continue his stud duties.

Although I had been having a good season with the horses, things weren't working out quite so well at Cabalva. I suppose the problem was that Harriet's presence there added another dimension, which upset the dynamics of the place. She and Revel were both very strong characters, so things were beginning to get a bit uncomfortable. Harriet was keen for us to set up on our own, but it was a difficult decision for me. I had always got on very well with Revel, and at Cabalva I had a secure job with a regular income. Life was comfortable in that respect, because everything was provided (my accommodation, the horsebox and so on) and it felt as if the yard was my own. Obviously, I was answerable to Revel, but she left me in charge of everything and I had complete responsibility. Revel was happy for me to accept rides on other people's horses, and I had some good horses coming along. Looking back on it now, I realise how lucky I was with the set-up at Cabalva, and if Harriet hadn't come into my life at that stage I probably would have stayed a lot longer. But then you have to move on sometimes, and on this occasion Harriet was certainly the catalyst.

By now my younger brother Graham had joined us at Cabalva and my father had become the farm manager there, so basically Revel was employing all my family. My father had always loved animals, and he had worked on a farm before getting the job of transporting mobile homes, so when the opportunity came up for him to take over as farm manager of the Cabalva estate he was delighted. I can remember that he checked with Graham and I before selling his mobile home business, in case either of us wanted to take it over, but by then we were both certain we wanted to make our careers with horses. The mobile home business would probably have been a safer bet!

Harriet and I moved out of Cabalva at the beginning of 1991 and went to work at Sam Barr's yard in Gloucestershire. I was 25 years old then and beginning to feel reasonably well established in the eventing world, but the move was initially quite a set back for me. The main problem was that Sam wasn't very keen for me to take on other people's horses, and although I had plenty of his horses to ride, most of them at that time were novices, so I had a very quiet year in terms of big competitions. Haig was one of only two horses that had come with me to Sam's yard. I was hoping to ride him at Badminton, but he damaged a tendon while competing at one of the spring events, so in the end we couldn't run him.

The set-up at the Barrs' yard was very different from Cabalva. Basically, I was there just to ride the horses and I was expected to work from 7.30am to 5pm, which was fine, but there was no flexibility. At Cabalva I had been used to planning my own day, and if I needed to go shopping for a couple of hours at lunchtime I could, and just work later that evening. It was up to me. I'm generally quite a tolerant person and I'm happy to accept most situations, but I did feel very restricted at the Welton Stud. Harriet, being the free spirit that she is, couldn't cope with it at all. I remember we used to have soup for lunch every day. The soup was made at the beginning of the week, and each day the leftovers were added to it, so sometimes it was thick soup, and sometimes it was like water. It took me a long time before I could face eating soup again after I'd left the place. By the end of that year we realised that our arrangement with the Barrs wasn't working, so we decided to rent some stables and set up on our own.

One advantage of moving to Gloucestershire was that, geographically, we were much more in touch with the eventing scene and felt more in the heart of it all. We had met some local people called the Goodwins, whose daughter had been having lessons with Harriet. They had a couple of stables and were quite interested in building a bigger yard, so when Harriet mentioned to them that we wanted to move, they went ahead with the project and built twelve new stables. I finished working for Sam in September, before the Goodwins' yard was ready, so we rented some stables from Audrey Brewer, who lived near Hartpury College. Over the winter I talked to a lot of people (mostly potential owners) about our move, so by early 1992, when the new stables were ready, we had quite a few horses to bring on. Basically we were happy to take anything and everything, because we were suddenly confronted with the need to pay rent and make our own living, which was quite frightening.

I suppose people thought that because Harriet was Rex Harrison's granddaughter she must have a lot of money, but she didn't. She had to make things pay, just as I did. After we had moved to our new stables, Harriet did inherit a bit of money, from her stepfather's side of the family, which helped us to get the yard up and running, though ultimately this money was the cause of some tension between us. I had one Advanced horse at the time, called Brownshill Boy, who was owned by Pat Harvey, the mother-in-law of our farrier. The horse had been ridden previously by Andrew Benny, but had had some time off because of an injury. I took him on at the beginning of the 1992 season, when we were incredibly busy getting the yard established, schooling horses for other people and doing a lot of teaching, so it was a serious setback when I had a fall from him and broke my ankle. We were competing at Dynes Hall, the home of the Hunnable family, in one of the first events of the season, and Brownshill Boy hit a fence and came down on his side, and the pressure of the stirrup iron cracked my ankle. I wasn't much use around the yard for a while.

That summer Harriet and I got married. We had a wonderful wedding at Holne in Devon, at her mother and stepfather's house: a lovely place on the edge of Dartmoor – very quiet and very beautiful. David Salmon is a keen gardener, and everything looked gorgeous. On the day of our wedding, June 13th, 1992, the weather was perfect, and I remember we had the sides of the marquee open so people could walk out into the garden. There was great mixture of guests: from Harriet's side there were actors, singers and writers, and from my side there was all my family – aunts, uncles and cousins – from a very different background. We were married in the Holne church and then had a very informal reception, with no speeches, which was probably a relief for my best man, Ian Silitch, who had come over from America for the wedding. Ian and I had remained close friends since my days working for him in the States, and he has played an important part in my life. He is a great guy with a wonderful temperament, and someone who I have always looked up to, so I was really pleased that he could be at the wedding.

There wasn't time for a honeymoon – we were in the middle of the eventing season – but earlier in the year Harriet and I had been on the holiday of a lifetime when we went to Thailand with her mother and stepfather. David is very keen on that part of the world and we stayed in a villa belonging to some friends of his on the island of Phuket, which was stunning. It was the most amazing place: the weather was flawless, the scenery was beautiful, the food was delicious and the people were so friendly. We had a brilliant time there, and I could hardly believe my eyes when I saw on the television the devastation caused by the tsunami. Patong had been such a colourful, vibrant place. We had wandered through the streets in the evenings, going to the bars and seeing the beautiful girls who'd call out to us, "We like you lots!" Harriet thought this was very funny. We had wonderful memories of the place, and to see the town reduced to rubble by the tsunami was very sad.

After our wedding in June it was straight back to work. My ankle was better, and Brownshill Boy was back in training with the aim of doing Burghley in September. This was my first four-star event for two and a half years, so I was delighted to go clear on the cross-country even though we hadn't done a great dressage. It was a tough cross-country course that year, and only one rider, Brynley Powell, completed it within the optimum time. I had 23.6 time penalties and also had two show jumps down on the final day, but we finished seventeenth overall.

Things gradually started to pick up again with my riding, and I was getting some more good horses, but after my slightly disappointing ride at Burghley it took another three years for me to get back to four-star level, and at times it seemed an uphill struggle. It didn't help that I had a couple of bad injuries during this period. The first was when I snapped a cruciate ligament in my knee jumping off a haystack. It wasn't a huge jump, probably only about six or seven feet, but I slipped when landing on some mud. My leg went back underneath me and the ligament gave way. The injury might not have happened, or not have been so bad, if I hadn't previously damaged the knee in a skiing accident two years earlier.

Ian Silitch had invited me out to the States for a couple of weeks around Christmas in 1989, and during that time we stayed with some clients of his who owned a ranch at Jackson Hole, Wyoming, and we all went skiing. Ian had been brought up in New Hampshire and had skied all his life, but I had never skied before and I was not reassured to discover that Jackson Hole is not a beginners' resort. Fortunately, Ian's girlfriend hadn't done any skiing either, so the two of us messed about on the one and only beginners' slope in the resort. We soon got a feel for it, and started going up the drag lifts, eventually progressing to a chair lift, which was terrifying.

We'd been given careful instructions on how to get on and off the chairlift, so when the thing came whipping round the corner we managed to get ourselves on it okay. I then spent the entire journey panicking about how high we were going and about how we were going to get off at the other end. We'd been told that the ground would come up to meet us and that we should make sure we got to the edge of the seat to push ourselves off. I remember reaching the top of the lift and thinking, "I've got to get off this thing." There was no way I was going round that wheel and back down again in the chair, because with my fear of heights it would be even worse going downwards. I was also worried that I would fall out of the chair, because there didn't seem to be a bar to hold us in. So as my skis touched the ground, I gave myself an almighty push, shot off the chair over the icy snow and straight into the couple who had just got off the lift in front us. I took them clean out.

After lengthy apologies I got myself sorted out, and even began to get the hang of the chairlifts. But the next day, Ian decided that we should progress further. He took me up another chairlift, which seemed to go even higher, and which then stopped for some reason while we were halfway up. So there we were, dangling high over the trees, with me already feeling sick with nerves, when Ian decided it would be a good laugh to start swinging the chair. That was all I needed. When we eventually got off the lift, the run looked incredibly steep. I started making my way tentatively down the mountain, and I wasn't doing too badly until I fell awkwardly with my knee back underneath me. The next morning my knee had swollen like a balloon, and although it settled down after a few days, I think that's when the initial damage was done.

After my slip from the haystack I didn't really appreciate what I had done to my knee, and because I was able to get going again after resting it for a while, I didn't do anything about it. But over time it became more and more unstable, and kept giving away, so eventually, at the end of 2003, I had keyhole surgery on it, which has been reasonably successful. Riding doesn't bother it, because the stirrup stabilises my leg, but I'm not so good at running and jumping.

The next injury was a lot more dramatic: I hit a tree and was knocked unconscious. This time at least I was riding a horse. It was on the cross-country at the novice event at Stowe School. As you rode through an avenue of trees, the track split in two, and at the divide there stood a tree. I had already been round the course on two other horses, and my next ride was a mare called Best By Miles. When we cantered rapidly towards this divide, I knew which way I was planning to go, but the mare suddenly decided she wanted to go on the other path and pulled across to it. I quickly turned my shoulders away from the tree and ducked my head to try and avoid it, but I still hit it almost full on, and I was out cold for few minutes.

It was strange, because although I was seriously concussed, I can vaguely remember a sense of panic around me while I was in the ambulance on the way to Stoke Mandeville hospital. Somehow I was aware that there was a lot of commotion, but my main sensation was of going on a long journey down a tunnel. It was all so easy: I was just gently drifting along, quietly and smoothly, enjoying the journey, and yet something in my subconscious told me that I must start to breathe. I can remember I started panting, and then everything around me calmed down. When I asked about it later, I was told that they were in a panic in the ambulance because they couldn't get enough oxygen into me. I'm sure that's the moment when I was drifting away.

All I can say is: if that's how you die, it's easy. I was definitely on the brink and it was an extraordinary experience. When I eventually came round the hospital staff were quite amused because I was so concussed that I was talking absolute rubbish. In my befuddled state I imagined I was trying to convince the doctor at the event that I was okay to ride. I was telling everyone that I was fine, and muttering about which fences I'd jumped on what horse, and babbling away about being fit enough to ride the next horse. I didn't remember a thing until the following day, when it all gradually came back to me. My shoulder was very painful, and X-rays revealed that I had seriously stretched the ligaments attaching the top of my arm to my shoulder blade. The injury gradually healed of its own accord, but I still have a large lump near my collarbone.

At the start of the 1994 season I was offered the ride on Welton Envoy, another of Sam Barr's horses, and I was still competing Haig, who had run well at Bramham the previous year. Both horses went to the British Championships at Gatcombe in the summer, and I was third in the Intermediate event on Welton Envoy and fifth in the Open Championships with Haig. Things were ticking along quite nicely, but I was still without a four-star horse, or even a horse with obvious four-star potential. That is, until I got the chance to ride New Flavour. The horse belonged to Nicky Coe, married to Sebastian Coe, who had won Badminton in 1990 on a horse called Middle Road. Nicky was expecting a baby in 1994 and had asked Angela Tucker to ride New Flavour for her. Angela had competed at quite a few events during the year, but the dates of Boekelo, a three-day event in Holland, clashed with her daughter's 21st birthday party. So Nicky asked me if I could go instead.

New Flavour was a fabulous horse. He had been very well trained by Nicky and then by Angela, so he was already going well in the dressage. I took him to a couple of Open Intermediate classes, one at Upton House, which we won, and another at Lulworth Castle, where we came third, and then we went to the three-star event at Boekelo and finished fourth, which was very exciting. He was in a different league from most of the other horses that I had at the time, so to have a ride like that was fantastic, and just what I needed. Unfortunately for me, Nicky took him back to ride herself at the beginning of the next season, but she started to have a few problems with him running out on the cross-country. He came back to me later that summer when Nicky was expecting another baby, but I didn't do a lot better. We had a run-out at Hartpury and Gatcombe, and then more trouble when we went back to Boekelo, so that winter I had him at my yard and spent a lot of time training him over narrow fences and corners, and taking him show jumping, until we'd built up a good rapport.

By this time I had also started riding a small, athletic horse called Capitano, a home-bred gelding belonging to Elf Reddihough. The horse had been ridden at four-star level by an Australian called Danny Wilson, who had been based in Scotland with Ian Stark, and when Danny went back to Australia, Elf offered the horse to me. Capitano was a brilliant cross-country horse, but he had a bit too much energy and enthusiasm, and he could really test my patience in the flatwork. He came to me at the beginning of 1995, and he had already done Badminton and Burghley the year before as an eight-year-old, so at last I had a horse that I could take to a four-star event. Three years after my last ride at Burghley with Brownshill Boy, I was finally back there again, and this time went so well that I even managed to impress the British team selectors. Not surprisingly, our dressage wasn't too good (49th at this stage), but Capitano flew round the cross-country to be one of only four horses to finish within the optimum time. The others were Kristina Gifford's General Jock and two horses ridden by New Zealand's Andrew Nicholson – Cartoon II and Buckley Province.

There was a big controversy surrounding Andrew's ride on Buckley Province. It seems that one of the stewards on the Roads and Tracks had nodded off for a while because he failed to tick the box to show that Andrew had passed his check point. On spotting the blank box on the score sheet, the technical delegate, Francois Lucas, immediately eliminated Nicholson without questioning him, or even consulting with the members of ground jury (the three overall judges). Not surprisingly, Andrew was furious, especially as he had gone into second place behind Kristina after the cross-country. As it turned out, he couldn't possibly have missed the check point concerned because it was in a straight line between two others, but it took until 7pm on cross-country day for the matter to be resolved, by which time tempers were fraying!

Andrew got his own back the next day by winning the event with a clear round in the show jumping on Buckley Province, and coming fourth on Cartoon II, but sadly Kristina dropped down to sixth place when General Jock had four fences down. Capitano had two down, but we finished tenth, and I think the selectors were particularly interested in him because the Atlanta Olympics were looming and there was already a lot of concern about how the horses would cope with the heat and humidity there. Capitano was a tough, wiry, athletic little horse who would be ideally suited to those conditions, so suddenly, having been without a four-star horse for three years, I was now being considered for Britain's team to go to the Atlanta Olympics. It's amazing how quickly things can change in this sport, for better or for worse.

So my competitive prospects were looking up, but at the same time my personal life was in turmoil. Harriet and I couldn't seem to agree on anything, and we were constantly arguing. The differences in our characters, which had been a source of attraction at the outset of our relationship, were now causing rifts. It didn't help that we were struggling to make our business work, which puts pressure on any relationship, however good. We both had rather different ideas on how we should run things. Harriet was prepared to take risks. She was a more daring person than me, and happy to live for today and worry about tomorrow when it comes. I was the conservative one, always wanting to hold back. I thought we should save what money we had for a rainy day and make sure we got things on a firmer footing. When Harriet went out and bought an expensive dressage horse, because she had decided that she wanted to make her career in dressage, I wasn't too happy. She had every right to do that, because what money we had was mostly hers, but while we were trying to run a business together, trying to make a go of things, it seemed to me like an unnecessary extravagance.

And so the tensions built up, the arguments continued and things went in a downward spiral. By the winter of 1995 we'd realised that our marriage wasn't going to work, and Harriet moved back down to Devon. In some ways it was a relief because at least we were no longer at loggerheads, trying to live under the same roof, but I also felt a sense of failure. I have often thought about it: why something that had been so good to start with, and such fun, should go so wrong. I had never felt about anyone the way I felt about Harriet, but you can't really change the sort of person that you are, and Harriet and I were two very different people.

The most important person in my life now is my fiancée Trina Lightwood. I think we get on so well because we are from quite similar backgrounds, and we are happy to work together as a partnership. There can easily be tensions when you are working with someone all the time, but we both have our separate areas of responsibility and we respect each other's space. We have built up a very strong relationship over the years, and I love Trina for the person she is. We work hard, but we have a lot of fun together and I have never been happier.

4
Olympic Aspirations

I couldn't have asked for a better start to 1996 as far as my riding was concerned. I had two horses, Capitano and New Flavour, heading for Badminton, and I now had three promising young horses at the yard: Cruiseway, Perryfields George and Shear H20. New Flavour had taken on board his winter lessons, and he went through the 1996 season without a single jumping fault across country, winning three out of his four spring events. Capitano was also going consistently well at the beginning of the season, and so, six years after last competing at Badminton on Welton Apollo, I was heading there again, this time with two horses and with the tantalising prospect of Olympic team selection.

There was obviously quite a lot of rumour and counter-rumour in the eventing world about my break-up with Harriet, but I just kept my head down and concentrated on the horses. The divorce settlement had to go through solicitors because we both had money tied up in the business at our yard at the Goodwins. The main problem was that Harriet's input, financially, had been greater than mine, so I had to pay her some money, but I didn't have any to give her. Eventually I managed to sell a horse in which I had a part interest, and so was able to pay her.

And so to Badminton, which produced a strange result for me. Capitano, the horse that both the selectors and I had thought was a likely contender for Atlanta, gave a lacklustre performance on the cross-country. He just wasn't his usual ball of energy, and we had a run-out at the steps, so we withdrew him after the event. It was very disappointing for his owner, Elf Reddihough, as well as for me, but at least I had a second ride to look forward to on New Flavour. He had done a good dressage which had put us in tenth place, and he gave me a fabulous ride cross-country – made it feel easy – and we finished within the optimum time to move up into fifth place. A clear show jumping round allowed us to creep up another place when Ian Stark had two fences down on Stanwick Ghost, and I landed up being the only British rider in the top five. Mark Todd won on Bertie Blunt, followed by another New Zealand rider Vaughn Jefferis, then the American David O'Connor, and Blyth Tait was in fifth place behind me – was I in good company!

"This job is easy," I said to myself, as I galloped round an Intermediate event on Matt Butler at Ragley Hall, the day after Badminton, "The best British rider at Badminton. No problem." Suddenly, the best British rider at Badminton was kissing the turf. I can't remember which fence I fell at, and I don't often feel very amused when I fall off, but we all had good laugh about this one. So now I have a rule that I never go to a competition the day after Badminton, and that's also why I knew it wouldn't be a good idea for me to ride the two novice horses on the cross-country at Solihull after I had been told that I'd won the gold medal in Athens. If I could fall flat on my face after coming fourth at Badminton, what would I do after winning an Olympic gold medal?

New Flavour's performance at Badminton just about assured our selection for Atlanta, which was very exciting. I had never been on the British team, and the only time I had ever represented Britain was in the 1989 European Championships at Burghley, when I rode as an individual. In 1996 there was a lot of talk was about how the horses would cope with the heat and humidity in Atlanta in July, and various studies were carried out to test their stress levels in these conditions. Because of the concern, the distances on the speed and endurance were reduced, and the cross-country took place as early as possible in the morning before it got too hot. It was the first time that watermist fans were used, which worked brilliantly for cooling down the horses – and it was nice for riders to stand underneath them as well. The organisers were under serious pressure to make to make sure there were no bad pictures of exhausted horses at the event, because the IOC (International Olympic Committee) was already making noises about dropping eventing from the Olympic Games. Added to that, the "Humane Society of the United States" had asked the IOC to cancel the three-day event, and had threatened to sue the Olympic Committee if any horses were "endangered". So everyone breathed a sigh of relief when both cross-country days passed without serious mishap.

There were two cross-country days because, for the first time, there was a separate team and individual competition. This was because the IOC had said that it couldn't give two Olympic medals (i.e. a team and individual award) for one performance. This seemed a bit mean when you consider how much we have to go through – dressage, cross-country and show jumping – just to get one medal, while other sportsmen, like gymnasts, can win medals for each separate performance whether it be on the bar, the mat or whatever. It was also a strange thing to do given that one of the main complaints about eventing in the Olympics was that it was very expensive to set up, and now in Atlanta they had to build two different cross-country courses: one for the team competition and one for the individual. Nations also had the dilemma of deciding which riders to put on the team and which to run as individuals. Should you put your best four on the team and aim for a team medal, or should you give your best three riders a shot at the individual medals? As it turned out, most countries put their teams first, but that had the effect of devaluing the individual event. In Atlanta, it was fortunate that the individual gold medal still went to a top class rider, Blyth Tait.

It was a miserable Olympics for Britain. The British riders had gone to Atlanta in the hope of getting at least one medal in eventing and one in the show jumping, but we all came back empty-handed. From the start, there hadn't been a great team spirit amongst the event riders, I think because the organisation and management weren't that good. Charlie Lane was our chef d'équipe, and the seven members of squad (four team and three individuals) were Ian Stark, William Fox-Pitt, Karen Dixon, Gary Parsonage, Mary King,

Charlotte Bathe and me, with Chris Hunnable as travelling reserve. We went out three weeks before the start of the event to acclimatise to the heat, which was probably a good idea, but the farm where we kept the horses didn't have very good facilities and the footing was a bit rough. Considering we were trying to prepare horses for an Olympic Games, the set-up was a bit disappointing. Keeping the horses fit and well occupied was difficult because we didn't go to any competitions and we didn't feel like galloping them much or jumping a lot of cross-country fences because of the rough ground. We ended up moving to the Olympic equestrian site, the Georgia Horse Park, a bit earlier than planned because the facilities there were better.

The most exciting part of the Games for me was attending the opening ceremony. It was a memorable night from the moment we began waiting for our turn to go into the stadium to when we finally got to our beds at about 2.30am. To start with, all the athletes were taken to a smaller stadium, where we assembled in our national groups and watched the entertainments of the opening ceremony on a big screen. It was an amazing feeling to be standing shoulder to shoulder with all these famous athletes – people that you'd seen on TV. I had never have dreamt that I would be mingling with them as part of Team GB. As the time grew near for us to parade around the stadium the excitement mounted. We were moved into a long tunnel, gradually getting nearer and nearer the entrance. At last it was our turn to go in and we surged up the ramp and into the stadium. I remember feeling a big adrenalin rush as we arrived in the stadium. It was amazing: so many people, banners, and flags – an absolute sea of colour – and the noise of cheering and clapping was overwhelming. We marched around the track, with Steve Redgrave holding the British flag, and then we waited in the middle of the stadium until finally Mohammed Ali lit the Olympic flame.

Filing out of the stadium at the end of it all seemed to take forever, and it was slightly nerve wracking. There had been some concerns about security, and later in the week there was a bomb explosion in downtown Atlanta. We certainly felt quite vulnerable as we queued to leave the stadium with thousands of other people. But no one minded about the wait. We were all so swept up in the moment: the excitement, the buzz and the emotion of it all. We were on cloud nine, and we didn't care what time we got to bed.

I didn't stay on cloud nine for long because the next day my Olympic dreams bit the dust. At the first horse inspection, when all the horses are trotted up in front of the Ground Jury (the three judges), New Flavour was held over. He was passed on the re-inspection, but because there was now a slight doubt about his soundness, the selectors decided not to risk putting him on the team. There was a possibility that I could have run as an individual, but they had to take a decision quite quickly on whether or not to bring in Chris Hunnable's horse, Mr Bootsie, for the individual trot up. As he was the reserve, he wasn't even at the Olympic site at that stage. Once they decided to bring him in, I had to go out. It was as simple as that. They didn't have a spare accreditation for the reserve, so I was stripped of mine and it was given to Chris, which was the most devastating part of the whole procedure. Suddenly I had become a non-person. I wasn't just out of the competition, I was kicked out of the venue as well. I felt as though I'd been found guilty of a crime and sent to jail.

It was very upsetting because Trina and I knew that the problem with New Flavour was just a small bruise on his foot, and with careful management he could probably have done the competition. Trina is absolutely brilliant at managing horses, and we have gone through three-day events successfully with similar problems with other horses, but I suppose the selectors weren't prepared to take the risk, even for me to run as an individual. What was really galling was that New Flavour was on such good form, and we were well aware that, because the best horses were running in the team competition, the individual competition was up for grabs. The way New Flavour had gone at Badminton, he must have stood a good chance of an individual medal, if only he had been allowed to run. I felt frustrated, disappointed, and excluded.

Fortunately, I was given a ticket to attend the event, and Rosemary Barlow, who does an amazing job organising a base for the

British Horse Trials Support Group at major championships, gave me access to their large, air conditioned tent, so I was able to meet up with people there. My mother and a couple of her friends had flown out just before the trot up, and Diana Fitzroy, a joint owner of New Flavour, was also there. The other members of the team were great, especially Chris Hunnable, who was obviously elated to be given the chance to ride but was really nice to me about it. But I still felt cut off from them and I got very little support from those responsible for the British squad, so when I was given the option of getting a flight straight back to England, rather than hanging around in Atlanta, I was tempted to take it. Mark Todd, whose horse had gone lame about a week before the start of the Games, had decided not to stay on, but he'd already experienced plenty of Olympic Games. This was my first, so in end I decided to stay and watch. I'm glad I did, because I was really quite naïve about it all, and I learnt a lot by just being there. Another time – and I was now determined that there would be another time – I would know what to expect: the security, the restrictions, and the different tensions that you might not have experienced or foreseen, which could perhaps affect your performance. The Olympic Games is so different from any other event. I was enthralled by it, and could now understand why riders were so keen to get there.

Sadly for our riders in Atlanta, things did not go well. In the team competition, Ian Stark had a fall from Stanwick Ghost at the first water complex on the cross-country, and William Fox-Pitt had a refusal with Cosmopolitan. Gary Parsonage (with Magic Rogue), who was riding on the team for the first time, and Karen Dixon on Too Smart, both went clear, but the team couldn't do better than fifth place. The individual competition wasn't any better. Mary King, who had been leading after the dressage, had a refusal on the cross-country with King William, and poor Charlotte Bathe, who had the best British cross-country round that day, found that The Cool Customer had torn a suspensory ligament. Chris Hunnable went clear, but he had a lot of time faults, and eventually finished tenth, which was the best British individual result .

Two good things came out of the Atlanta disappointment. One

was that I came home wanting to go to another Olympics, and the other was that I started going out with Trina who had been grooming for me for the last two years. Trina had initially come to work for Harriet and me for a year while she was studying for her National Diploma in Equine Studies at Moreton Morrell College in Warwickshire. When she'd finished her course, she came back to work for us permanently. There can't be much that Trina doesn't know about managing event horses, and she always comes with me to the major events. Once I've finished riding a horse on the cross-country, it goes straight to her. I just give her the information she needs, such as whether the going was very hard, if I think the horse might have jarred itself, or knocked its stifle on a fence. She then treats the horse accordingly, dealing with any possible problems before they become more serious. To her credit I have never been unsuccessful in presenting a horse on the final day of a three-day event.

By the time we got back from Atlanta we'd been away for over a month, so there was some catching up to be done at home. Capitano was back on form, and I took him and another good horse called Cruiseway up to Thirlestane Castle for the Scottish Open Championships. Cruiseway belonged to Alan Spiers, and had come to me as a four-year-old to be broken in. I had come third with him at Bramham in June, before going to Atlanta, and at Thirlestane he came a credible fourth in the "Gents" Advanced section. Capitano came eighth. Still in Scotland, I took Perryfields George to his first two-star CCI, at Blair Castle, where he came third, so all in all my trip north was a successful one.

Perryfields George was a fabulous horse. Martin Sadler had bought him as a three-year-old, and because he was so good looking he took him to Robert Oliver to see if he might make a show hunter. Robert thought he wouldn't quite make the grade, but he did think he would make a good event horse. To which Martin's response was, "What's an event horse, and who do I send him to?" Martin was into racing and was also a keen hunting man, but he had never been involved in eventing. Robert, who lived only a few miles from the Goodwin's yard, where I was still based, told him that he should send the horse to Leslie Law. "Who's she?" was his response to that suggestion. But not long afterwards Liam Kearns, one of the local vets, was at Martin's yard and saw Perryfields George. Martin asked him if he could recommend someone to send the horse to and Liam mentioned me again. After two recommendations, I think Martin got the hint. He rang me up and asked if I'd like to take on the horse.

Perryfields George was only four then and hadn't done anything, but this was in 1993, not long after Harriet and I had set up on our own, so I was glad to take him on. In fact, he was a very exciting prospect: he looked gorgeous and he moved very well. Since then Martin has been one of my regular owners. Another owner, whose involvement was to have a huge effect on my career, was Jeremy Lawton. I met him the following year, through the dealer Brian Lusk, who was based at Mill Hill. Jeremy, who lives in North London not far from Brian, had some show jumpers with him, which were being ridden by Roddy Dean. One of these horses wasn't really working out as a show jumper, so Brian suggested they send it eventing and he gave Jeremy my phone number. I agreed to take on the horse, a five-year-old gelding, but he hadn't got anything like as much potential as Perryfields George.

We entered him for the Burghley Young Event class at Hartpury a few weeks after I'd had him, and Jeremy came to watch. He didn't go too badly, and we finished about half way down the class, but I'd already made my own assessment of the horse, and I didn't think he was worth persevering with. My policy has always been to be open with owners and not to pretend that their horse has got something when it hasn't, so when we were having a cup of tea together in the lorry afterwards, I asked Jeremy where he saw himself going as an owner within eventing. He said he wanted a horse at the top of the sport. "Well," I said, "the horse you've been watching today is not going to be the one!"

His response to that was that we should sell him and find a horse that would go to the top. This was a fantastic opportunity for me; I could buy a young horse of my choosing, bring it on myself and hopefully take it to the top of the sport. By the end of the year I had tracked down a lovely grey gelding that Roland Fernyhough had bought out of Ireland as a three-year-old. Roland had done a bit of show jumping with him, but didn't feel that he was going to make a top class show jumper and so was marketing him as an eventer. My meeting with Roland was the start of a regular association with him, and since then he has helped me with my show jumping and I have bought and sold horses through him. At the time he was married to Nicky Caine, Michael Caine's daughter (who I also do business with now) selling horses to Tracey Bowman in California.

We bought Shear H2O as he was rising five. Jeremy, whose insurance company is called Shearwater, gave him his name, but we usually call him by his stable name Solo. He was a brilliant horse to bring on. He took it all in his stride, and in the autumn of 1996, when he was only a six-year-old, I took him to the two-star CCI in Pau, France, where he finished ninth, so at least 1996 ended on a good note.

5
A Year to Forget

1997 had the potential to be my best year so far. I had a yard full of good horses, two of them heading for Badminton. New Flavour and Capitano were my Badminton rides, and again they turned the tables on their expected performances. I was the first competitor out on the cross-country with Capitano, and he felt fantastic – absolutely pinged around the course – but as we'd been placed 69th after the dressage, there wasn't much hope of winning. He went clear in the show jumping and we finished sixteenth, which represented the biggest climb up the scoreboard of any competitor, and so we were awarded the Glentrool Trophy. I sometimes wonder if there should be an opposite prize to the Glentrool Trophy, for riders who drop the furthest down the scoreboard on the final day. Poor Ian Stark, who had been in the lead after the cross-country, plummeted to thirteenth place when Stanwick Ghost had five fences down, handing the Mitsubishi Trophy to the American rider David O'Connor.

Obviously my main hope of a good result at Badminton had been with New Flavour, after his performance here the previous year. He did a reasonable dressage, but by the time we had got to the Huntsman's Halo on the cross-country, five fences from home, he'd had enough, and after one refusal here, I retired him. He just didn't feel right. It was a massive disappointment for the horse's owners, the Coes and Diana Fitzroy, and also for me. It transpired that New Flavour had damaged a tendon and would have to have a year off, so it was decided to retire him from eventing.

After Badminton, it was clear that I wasn't going to be selected for that year's European Championships, but at least Perryfields George was coming on well, and he did a couple of three-star events – Bramham and Blenheim – finishing seventh and fourth. I also had a good two-star horse called Matt Butler, owned by Diana Fitzroy, who went well at the two Irish CCIs, Blarney Castle and Necarne Castle. Shear H2O, who was only seven years old, had already been to his first Advanced events and was going brilliantly, so I decided to enter him for one of the Advanced sections at Gatcombe in August. Capitano would do the Open Championships there. Little did I know that this was to be Capitano's last event and that, in the space of three months, I would have lost the ride on both my four-star horses. As if that wasn't bad enough, I was about to take a personal battering that made me question very seriously my future in the sport.

At Gatcombe, Capitano was lacking his usual enthusiasm on the cross-country, and by the time we reached the park bowl, in front of the house, he felt as if he was running low on energy. I wasn't sure what to do. I knew that the steep hills at this event make the course very testing and horses don't always feel quite as full of running as usual. Capitano was still jumping well enough, and by the time we had run down the hill and through the water complex we were near the end of the course, so I thought I would just keep him cantering to the finish. As we landed from jumping the table, one fence from home, he suddenly veered off to the left, lurched through the string on the side of the course and fell down. It was the most awful feeling. My first thought was that he'd broken a leg, because as he landed his legs seemed to give way, and his momentum took him through the string. But he hadn't broken a leg: he had collapsed and died.

I was devastated. I didn't know what to do with myself. I suppose I was in a state of shock. I felt empty inside, but I also kept thinking, "Why did this happen?" The next day I was still struggling to come to terms with it all when I discovered that British Eventing wanted to hold an enquiry into the accident, to investigate if I had been "over-pressing a tired horse". To me this was like pouring salt on a wound. Obviously, it didn't help that the horse died where he did, in the full glare of publicity at the Open Championships, but the news of the investigation stunned me.

I realised this meant that I would have to go before an enquiry and explain what happened, but I was very naïve about the whole procedure. I was expecting to just go along to the enquiry and defend myself on my own, and I think if I had done that they would have made mincemeat of me. Luckily, owners and friends came to the rescue, offering help and advice. Without their support, the enquiry could have gone against me, which probably would have been the final straw. I was already close to giving up my eventing career because of the hurt caused by the gossip, and the muck-spreading that was going on behind my back. I suppose people were bound to think the worst, but what really surprised me was that one or two very influential people in the sport were deliberately canvassing for opinions against me, trying to get others to agree that I had over-ridden the horse. It was very upsetting, and at times I felt that I just didn't want to carry on any more. It didn't seem worth it. This sport is tough enough without having to deal with that kind of pressure.

Elf Reddihough, the owner of Capitano, her father, Capt. Douglas Mann, Jeremy Lawton and Martin Sadler had all been at Gatcombe and had seen what happened. Together with my vet, John Killingbeck, they helped me put my case together and they acted as witnesses on my behalf. Throughout the whole episode they were absolutely brilliant, and they all came to the enquiry. By then, we had the results of the post-mortem, which showed that Capitano had had an aneurism – a burst blood vessel that had caused his lungs to fill with blood. It can happen any time, but unfortunately for me it happened at Gatcombe. Even if I had pulled him up, he would have died on the way back to the lorry. When we saw the video footage at the enquiry it did look as if the horse was very tired, and I was riding him strongly, but I never used my whip.

The enquiry acquitted me of any wrongdoing, which was a huge relief, but of course people still remembered the incident and for a while the mud stuck. It didn't help that Shear H2O, who was beginning to make his mark on the eventing scene, is very much a one-paced horse, so to achieve the speeds required on the cross-country I often have to push him on a bit. I need to keep after him and keep chivvying him along, and people watching are probably thinking, "Oh, there goes Leslie Law, pressing another tired horse!"

I may have been acquitted, but the incident certainly gave me a wake-up call. I understood the need for British Eventing to hold an enquiry because it has a responsibility to look after the image of the sport, but I certainly found it very difficult to ride competitively for some time afterwards. Ultimately, it made me a stronger person and, I hope, a better rider and competitor.

There is a fine line between wanting to win and being over-competitive and, unlike in most other sports, being over-competitive in eventing can be dangerous or it can be detrimental to a horse's welfare. Looking back on it all, I think that if faced with a similar situation now I would certainly pull a horse up sooner; but I also think that the people in charge at British Eventing could have handled the whole thing very differently. The enquiry, with all the personal anguish that it caused, came and went; yet in spite of what had happened at Gatcombe nobody from BE gave me any advice about my riding or about how to deal with this type of incident with a horse. That has made me want to help other people, particularly younger riders. Instead of riders being given a hard time when they are a bit too competitive, they need to be given advice, to be made aware of the possible consequences of their actions, so that they don't fall into the same trap as I did. British sportsmen and woman are often criticised for not being competitive enough, so when you get someone who does have that competitive edge, it needs to nurtured, not stamped on.

As a final blow to an already bad year, Perryfields George was sold to Italy. I was heartbroken when that happened. George was such a lovely stamp of a horse – a 16.3 hands full thoroughbred with a fantastic temperament – and I had brought him on since he was four, taking him through the grades and building up his trust. Unlike Capitano and New Flavour, who had come to me as made horses, George was the first really good one that I had made myself. In 1997 we had a very successful year, coming seventh at Bramham in June and fourth at Blenheim in September, and he looked ready to fill the shoes of the two four-star horses that I had just lost. He would certainly have been my next Badminton horse, and I already had that in my sights for the following year. But his owner, Martin Sadler, was offered a serious amount of money for him, and as he wasn't particularly interested in having a horse at the top level, he decided to sell. He made sure I was well rewarded for my part. Martin has always been very honest and open about what he is planning to do, and he has remained one of my most supportive owners. He only came into the sport because Robert Oliver had told him that George might make a good event horse, and what he enjoys most about eventing is coming along to the grass roots competitions and watching young horses being produced.

It was Martin who offered Trina and me our new premises. By the end of 1997, we had outgrown the Goodwin's place. We had about twelve boxes at their yard, and we'd managed to rent another six stables a few hundred yards away, but the logistics of taking food and equipment down the road every day was a nightmare. Martin had a bigger yard, and he was happy to build a few extra boxes to bring the total to twenty. He also had two cottages that we could use, which meant that the grooms didn't have to live in a house with us any more. It was sad to leave the Goodwins, who had been so good to us, but it made sense to move, and so at the beginning of 1998 we settled into our new base at Perryfields Farm near Inkberrow in Worcestershire. I was looking forward to putting the previous year behind me and making a fresh start.

6
Moving On

One of the few good things about 1997 had been that Shear H2O (Solo), the seven-year-old grey gelding owned by Jeremy Lawton, had been going brilliantly. Jeremy was so pleased with his progress that he offered to buy another horse for me to ride, so we rang up Roddy Dean, who had ridden show jumpers for him, to ask if he knew of anything. Roddy had moved back to Ireland by then, so Jeremy and I went over to stay with him and to have a look at some young horses. Roddy had seen a five-year-old gelding jumping at some local shows who was by Stan The Man, the same sire as Solo, so we were intrigued to see him. He did remind me in some ways of Solo, but he was a finer type, more thoroughbred, and actually better looking. When I had first seen Solo I'd had slight reservations about him because he was quite a butty little horse as a youngster, and I was worried that he wasn't quite thoroughbred enough in type. Yet when I rode him he gave me such a good feel that he was totally convincing, more convincing than the new horse we were trying. Nevertheless, I liked this five-year-old enough to want to buy him, and Jeremy dreamed up another good name to reflect his company: we called him Shear L'Eau, and nicknamed him Stan, after his sire. Jeremy decided to syndicate a part-share of Stan, and Elf Reddihough, Steve Green and Dick Bushnell all joined the syndicate.

It wasn't until I was going through Shear L'Eau's papers, some time later, that I realised he was actually a full brother to Solo, which was a wonderful discovery. They were both out of a mare called

Starry Knight. Stan turned out to be slightly easier to look after than his older brother, but more excitable to ride. He was good at bucking, and still is sometimes, and can often take a fair bit of persuading to settle down and concentrate on his work. He has a lot of talent, more than his brother, and he knows it. Solo, on the other hand, has always been a bit more serious about his work. As a youngster he was quite a bolshie character who liked things on his own terms and wouldn't be adverse to pulling a few faces and telling you where to go if he didn't like something. Initially, he was a nightmare to have on the yard: when we turned him out he would jump from one paddock to the next, and when he wanted to come in he would jump the gate. You could tell when he was going to do it; he'd just set his canter in a rhythm and keep coming. At the Goodwin's yard we had a large bank that ran down from the stables to the arena, and one day he leapt off the top of the bank straight into the arena. His attitude was one of complete independence, and he'd just say to himself, "I think I'll go here now!" And off he went.

Solo's greatest asset is that he is such a competitor. He might give you a hard time outside the arena, but once he's in there he will always perform competitively. That is what has made him such a great horse, and it certainly helped him to make rapid progress in his eventing career. With hindsight, I probably moved him on a bit quickly. If I were to produce him all over again, I don't think I would do things quite the same, but you learn by your mistakes. Solo excelled as a six-year-old, and I took him to the two-star CCI in Pau, France, which is quite a big competition for a horse of that age. Nevertheless, he did very well there, finishing ninth. The following year, 1997, he was placed in all his Advanced classes, winning two of them, and we ended the season with an eighth place at Le Lion d'Angers, in France. He hadn't put a foot wrong in his competitive career so far. As far as Jeremy Lawton was concerned, this eventing lark was marvellous: everything was just plain sailing and red rosettes. It was a bit of a shock, then, when things went belly up for Solo and me in Punchestown, Ireland, the following year.

The cross-country at Punchestown, a three-star event, was certainly a tough one, but I felt that Solo was more than ready for it.

The problem came at the water complex, where the distance between the obstacle into the water and the bank in the middle of the water seemed a bit unfair. It certainly didn't work for us: Solo tripped up the bank and I fell off. At that point I panicked slightly, I leapt back on and rushed around to the alternative as fast as possible, too fast for either of us to be properly organised, so we went splat over that as well, and that was the end of Punchestown. It gave a bit of a wake-up call to horse and rider, and a serious wake-up call to poor Jeremy, who couldn't believe that something had actually gone wrong! It wasn't the last of our problems, but at least we had good runs at two more three-star CCI's that year – Luhmuhlen in July, where we came eleventh, and Achselschwang in September, where we finished third.

By now Cruiseway, who had had the previous year off because of a leg injury, was back in work, and I took him to Badminton in the spring of 1998, which was the year Chris Bartle won on Word Perfect. A few weeks before Badminton, David Foster, one of Ireland's top international event riders, had been killed in a fall at a one-day event. His horse had hit some rails, somersaulted over the fence and landed on top of him. The accident had given us all quite a shock. It wasn't the first time that a rider had been killed in the sport, but it was the first death of a high profile, international competitor. David had been an exceptionally good rider, and suddenly it dawned on us that even the best riders could be killed. However careful and competent you were, things could still go wrong. I didn't know David well, but he was very popular, and he had a wife and three young children.

Obviously, when something like this happens you do question your own involvement with the sport. Equally, though, you are aware that people die in car accidents every day and it doesn't stop you driving. Although I was certainly affected by David's death, I wasn't going to stop riding. Eventing is a risk sport – I'm not under any illusions about that – but I love the challenge of it. If I ever got to the stage where I started thinking too hard about the possible consequences of what I was doing, it would be time to stop doing it.

I think most of the riders were feeling a bit subdued at Badminton because of David's death. It wasn't a good Badminton for me anyway. Cruiseway didn't go well on the cross-country, and after a couple of stops about two thirds of the way round the course, I decided to retire him. It was pity, because he had been a very promising horse, but after his year off he didn't come back with the same enthusiasm. He seemed to have lost his edge. He did manage a tenth place at Blenheim that autumn, but I felt that he wasn't really enjoying it anymore, and we decided to take him out of eventing. So I was without a four-star horse, and my attempt to get back on the British team, which that year went to Pratoni, in Italy, for the World championships, was looking like a very long-term project.

I was determined to ride at Badminton again in the following year, and as Solo had gone so well at his last three-day event in Achselschwang, I felt he was ready for it, even though he was only nine. I also had Diana Fitzroy's horse, Matt Butler, entered, attempting his first four-star event. Unfortunately, 1999 was a very wet year at Badminton, and one thing I found out pretty quickly was that Solo does not like muddy, wet ground. We'd already come off the steeplechase with a lot of time faults, so I knew he wasn't enjoying the going, but I certainly wasn't expecting to have two falls on the cross-country. That seemed more than my fair share. The first came at what was called the Challenger Bank – a big Irish bank with a ditch in front of it and a large, hanging log on the back of it. On the approach to the bank, the horses had the impression that there was a huge drop off the far side of it, over the log, but in fact the ground sloped gently away behind it, so it actually had quite a kind landing. Solo slipped slightly as he landed on the bank, and then he fell over the log. It was a big fall for both of us, because we were at the top of the bank when it happened.

I got back on, but three fences later I was on the ground again. There was a bounce over two roll-top fences going into the lake, and as we landed over the first of these, Solo shot left and I went right, so then it was time to call it a day. I had already retired Matt Butler, my first ride, when we had had two refusals at the Colt Walls, six fences from the end. I think at that point he'd decided enough was enough. It certainly wasn't my best Badminton, but there had been worse problems than mine. Among the various injuries and incidents was the dramatic moment when Stuart Tinney, the Australian rider, lost control of his horse after coming out of the Lake, and jumped over the chestnut palings into the crowd of spectators, with the result that two of the spectators had to be taken to hospital. Frenchay Hospital, in Bristol, was kept particularly busy on cross-country day: as well as injured spectators, three riders were also taken there – Eric Smiley and Joanne Jarden (both Irish riders), and Polly Phillipps, who was knocked unconscious after a bad fall.

Polly's fall had ua all worried, but it looked worse than it really was. Fortunately, she was only unconscious for a few minutes, and suffered nothing more than a broken collarbone. There was worse to come, however, and within four months Polly was dead. Badminton heralded the start of what was probably the worst year in the history of eventing – a year of organisational blunders and tragic accidents. It began with a certain amount of ill feeling among the riders at Badminton because most of us thought that the cross-country course was too twisty and had been measured too tight, so the time was going to be very difficult to achieve. On the day, the progressively wetter conditions made it even more testing, and no one came near the optimum time, not even those riders like Ian Stark and Mark Todd who had gone out on the course earlier in the day before it started raining heavily.

There was also dissatisfaction with the new scoring system, which had just been introduced. The idea had been to simplify the scoring so that it would be easier for spectators to understand, but in the end it was so unpopular that the old system was reinstated for 2000. At Badminton, the new system was put into use for the first time at a British three-day event: there was no multiplying coefficient for the dressage scores, and on the cross-country one penalty was allocated for every second over the time, instead of the usual 0.4 penalties for each second. So now the dressage scores became much more spread out and influential (they ranged from 56 to 133 at Badminton that year) and there was even more emphasis, certainly psychologically, on a rider's cross-country speed. It all led to some rather strange scores, and when Ian Stark came in for the show jumping on the final day he had four fences in hand over Mark Todd, so his victory was almost a forgone conclusion.

In addition to the problems at Badminton, there were other bad vibes on the eventing grapevine. News had been released that Polly Phillipps' horse, Coral Cove, whose good performance the previous year at the World Championships in Pratoni, had helped Britain secure the bronze medal, had tested positive from a routine random sample taken immediately after the show jumping in Pratoni. This was potentially disastrous for Britain, because if we were to lose the bronze medal the team would not qualify for the Sydney Olympics.

After my falls at Badminton, I decided to take Solo straight on to Chatsworth the following week to restore his confidence, which worked well because he finished third in the three-star CIC. We then went to the Bramham three-day event, in Yorkshire, which is a three-star competition and not as tough as Badminton, and I thought a run there would be good for both of us. Polly had also decided to take Coral Cove to Bramham for the same reason, and while we were at the event the furore over her horse's positive drugs test moved to a new level. The British team had now been stripped of its bronze medal following an unsuccessful attempt by the British Horse Trials Association (now British Eventing) to appeal against the case, and on the Friday of Bramham both Andy Bathe, the team vet, and Giles Rowsell, the chairman of selectors and chef d'équipe, resigned.

Polly had been given a one-month suspension by the FEI, but because she was allowed thirty days to appeal against her suspension, she could still run at Bramham. It was not at all clear where the blame lay for the problems in Pratoni, and some riders thought it was wrong that Polly should continue competing when other people had already suffered the consequences of the positive drug test. They felt that she ought to be taking her share of responsibility for it, and there was a strong feeling of resentment towards her at Bramham. I didn't know her very well, so I kept well out of it, though that doesn't mean that I wasn't as keen as the next person to know what had really happened in Pratoni. The general mood was already gloomy because only two weeks earlier another event rider had been killed. Peta Beckett, who had had a last-minute call up to compete as an individual at the World Games in Pratoni, where she finished 24th on a horse called Watermark, had died after a fall with a novice horse at Savernake horse trials. 1999 was beginning to look like another year to forget.

At least for me, Bramham was a good experience. Solo had clearly put his Badminton memories behind him and he went brilliantly to give me my first three-day event win at three-star level. I was delighted for Jeremy, because after Punchestown and Badminton he must have been beginning to wonder what was going wrong. As far as I was concerned, it totally reaffirmed my belief in the horse. I knew that Solo had his critics, because he often looks lacklustre on the cross-country, but this is because he never really takes up the bridle and runs. He's the same from the moment he comes out of the start box until the end of the course. I know when I'm sitting on him that he doesn't feel tired, and Bramham certainly restored my faith in him.

However, my victory there was completely overshadowed by the Coral Cove saga. Polly had finished second, so she was at the final press conference with me when a group of riders came into the back of the press tent. When one of the journalists asked Polly if she had found it difficult to compete in such a hostile environment, Mark Todd interrupted the press conference by angrily demanding an explanation from Polly about the positive drug test on her horse. Polly couldn't really say anything because her appeal against her one-month suspension was still ongoing. It was all very tense, and the press had a field day over the whole incident. "Angry Riders Turn on Phillipps" was among the headlines in the next day's papers. The fact that I'd won the event was much less newsworthy.

Throughout the 1999 season British eventing seemed to lurch from one disaster to the next. About two weeks after Bramham, Michael Allen, the chairman of the BHTA, resigned, and a week later Bridget Parker, a board member and selector, offered her resignation. That was followed in a few days by the resignation of Clarke Willis, the managing director of BHTA – all as a result of the Coral Cove affair – so by then there weren't many people left to run the association. One good thing that emerged from it all was that Jane Holderness Roddam was elected as the new chairman of the BHTA, and, because so many people had gone, she was able to bring in some new faces and make a fresh start. It must have been a hell of a job to come into though. It could not have been a worse time for British eventing, but Jane dealt with it all incredibly well, and she earned a lot of respect from the riders and from the press who were reporting on all the gloomy stories.

The next blow was the death of the Australian rider Robert Slade, who was killed at the Wilton Park Horse Trials at the end of June, and then there was yet another fatal accident in August. At Thirlestane Castle, in Scotland, riders short listed for the British team for September's European Championships in Luhmuhlen were having their final trial when the accident occurred. It was bad enough that another rider should die while competing at an event, but that it should be Polly Phillipps was uncanny. It was another terrible day for the sport, and the organisers of Thirlestane immediately cancelled the remainder of the event.

Polly's funeral was held on the Friday of Burghley. Unbelievably, there was another death the next day. The eventing world seemed to be in a permanent state of shock. Simon Long, in his first attempt at Burghley, died in a fall at the twentieth fence, the Sunken Water, which was a difficult, coffin-style complex. Blyth Tait also had a very bad fall at the same fence and broke his leg.

I had had a good round on Shear H2O until we got to the Podiums near the end of the course. These were three offset, rounded palisades with a stride in between each one (the previous year there had only been a bounce between each one). I didn't get my line quite right and Solo just ducked out of the last one. It was an annoying forty penalties (we were still under the temporary new scoring system), and with some time faults to add we dropped down to fourteenth place after the cross-country, but I was delighted with the way Solo had coped with the course. A clear show jumping round the following day put us into tenth place. Mark Todd won the event on Diamond Hall Red, and was also third on Word for Word.

One more disaster was to hit eventing before the end of the year:

the death of a talented young Irish rider called Peter McLean, who had just joined the Lawrence David team and looked to have promising career ahead of him. He died after falling at a fence at the Somerleyton Horse Trials in Suffolk only two weeks after Burghley. Five riders had died in five months. There was, not surprisingly, a lot of debate about the safety of eventing, and whether or not these deaths were just freak accidents – an unlucky patch for the sport – or whether the courses were becoming too difficult. A committee was set up to investigate ways of making the sport safer, and as a result cross-country courses now have collapsible rails on some of the obstacles.

At least the season concluded with a welcome victory for the British riders in Luhmuhlen, where they won both the team and individual gold medals. Pippa Funnell had become the new European champion and Britain, under the directorship of the new chairman of selectors, Mandy Stibbe, had now qualified for the Sydney Olympics. At last there was light visible at the end of the tunnel. I felt quietly confident that my own fortunes were also on the turn. Shear L'Eau had been steadily progressing throughout the year; he had won the two-star CCI at Blarney Castle in June, and was eleventh at Le Lion d'Angers, another two-star CCI, in October. Shear H2O had gone well at Bramham and Burghley, and if we could impress the selectors at Badminton next spring, there might be a chance of getting to the Sydney Olympics.

7

A Silver Lining

Early in 2000 I was one of eleven riders to be included in the "World Class Performance Eventing Squad", which had been set up as a result of the Lottery Sports Fund. It was the first time we had had so much financial backing for our training, but it came with a few strings attached, one being that there were certain government-funded personnel allocated to each sport whom we were expected to make use of and to incorporate into our training programme. So at the usual squad training session at the beginning of the season, we found there were a few extra people around – a nutritionalist and a sports psychologist, for example. This was all quite new for us and, to be honest, I think some of us decided it was a bit of a joke. We couldn't really see what relevance these people had for riders. What they were suggesting obviously worked for other athletes, but we had horses to consider as well. Nutritionally, most of us spent much more time worrying about what our horses were eating than whether or not we were consuming too many Mars Bars or crisps in a day.

As for the sports psychology, it didn't help that the people they brought in didn't really understand the sport. It's all very well turning a negative into a positive, but if you know your horse is a bit unreliable on ditches and you're heading towards the Vicarage Vee at Badminton, that's an awfully big negative to convert into a positive. I agree that if you ride positively it does transmit to your horse (and vice-versa if you are negative) but we were already aware of most of these things and we didn't see how these people were going to help us. Eventing was new territory for sports psychologists, and we didn't make things easy for them. It is much better now: the psychologists are more in tune with the sport, and with younger riders coming through it is easier to train them from the start. I felt quite sorry for our psychologist at those early sessions because she was up against some well established riders, who had done things their own way for so long that it was always going to be an uphill struggle to persuade them to make changes. There were people like Ian Stark, Mary King, Karen Dixon, Tina Gifford and Jeanette Brakewell on the squad. My brother Graham and Rodney Powell were also there, so we all had a bit of a laugh about it.

I can remember we had to keep food diaries, and we had lectures on not drinking too much tea or coffee, and not stopping off at Burger King on the way home from an event! It was all very well telling us that it was bad to go for long periods without food, but when you're at an event with four or five horses to ride, you don't get much time to eat. All this was a steep learning curve for the riders and the sports science team. I suppose some of it sunk in and was quite useful, but the funniest thing was that when we finally got to Sydney, where of course we were supposed to be on this healthy food and strict fitness regime, we found ourselves staying in a hotel called the Panthers, which had a 24-hour bar and casino attached to it. It tickled our sense of humour, when we'd been told that we should steer clear of alcohol and cigarettes, and get plenty of sleep each night, that we should land up in a hotel with every vice you could wish to take up, available round the clock.

The most useful thing that I have taken away from the sports psychology instruction is the use of visualisation. The idea is that you go over in you mind exactly what you are planning to do, for example on the cross-country. You visualise yourself approaching and jumping every fence around the course; you think about how you are going to ride that fence, and how the horse will jump it. Then you visualise every possible scenario – things that could go wrong – and you imagine yourself correcting mistakes or sorting out possible problems. Finally, you go round the whole course again with a "perfect" round: in other words, you visualise yourself getting everything right. Then you hope your visualisation becomes reality.

The other useful thing is to be able to turn your mistakes into a positive learning process, rather than negative thoughts of disappointment, which do nothing but sap your confidence. I think I had more or less learnt to do that by the time we were being offered help from sports psychology. I'd certainly made plenty of mistakes in my time. Of all of us on the squad, I think Pippa Funnell probably benefited the most from the sports psychology training. She had had a tough time breaking through to the senior ranks after a successful spell in juniors and young riders, and I think her confidence had taken a dive. But she never gave up. She worked incredibly hard and she used sports psychology to boost her confidence, which made all the difference to her performances.

Chris Bartle was also on the squad, which was quite strange because he was our dressage trainer, but it didn't seem to bother him. Flatwork has always been my weakest link. It's the most unnatural phase for me, and Chris gave me a lot of help with it, teaching me a huge amount. Kenneth Clawson helped with our show jumping, and Yogi Breisner was now the overall team trainer. Being on the squad for training was certainly a benefit, but my place on the team for Sydney was by no means assured and would depend on achieving a good result at Badminton. Fortunately, that's exactly what I did.

I had the same two horses at Badminton as I'd had the year before – Matt Butler and Shear H2O. Matt Butler did an even better dressage test than Solo, and by the end of the first two days I was the best British rider in the top four, lying in third place. Solo was equal eleventh, so we were quite well placed at the start of the cross-country. The going was much better this time, though it was still a bit boggy and holding in places. I was the first competitor out on the course with Solo, which didn't bother me; if anything it was a good thing for me because it meant that I wouldn't be able to have second thoughts about any of my plans after watching other horses go. We had a wonderful round: Solo just romped over the course, and he finished full of running and well within the optimum time, confounding those critics who had said he was tired the previous year when we had been eliminated. I was delighted because there had been a lot of narrow fences and arrowheads, and Solo had been accurate and honest at every fence. My only negative thought as I crossed the finishing line was that the time had been too easy to achieve, and that plenty of other people were also likely to finish without time penalties, which would make my score less competitive.

To my surprise, I held on to the lead until nearly the end of the day, when Mary King, who had been fifth after the dressage, came home within the optimum time on Star Appeal and overtook me. I slipped down to second, and Rodney Powell was lying third on Flintstone. Only seven horses finished within the optimum time, so it hadn't been as easy as I thought. Unfortunately, with my second ride, Matt Butler, who was one of the last to go on the cross-country, I had another disappointing Badminton round. He stopped at the Bank, the same fence where I'd had a fall on Solo the previous year, and then he had another stop at the Vicarage Vee, where we retired.

It was slightly disappointing to have a fence down with Solo in the show jumping the following day, but it didn't affect my position, and we finished second behind Mary King. It was my best ever Badminton result, and it couldn't have come at a better time. Barring any disasters between now and September, I had secured my place on the squad for Sydney. After a gap of four years, when I'd had my disastrous trip to Atlanta, I was once again selected for the British team and heading for another Olympic Games. Perhaps this time I would actually get to ride for the team.

The build up to Sydney was a lengthy process. The horses had to spend six weeks in quarantine, just over two weeks in this country and then the rest out in Australia, before the Games started. I seemed to spend my life disinfecting myself and climbing in and out of special tracksuits and white coats. Luckily, our base in England was at Eddy Stibbe's yard at Waresley Park, which couldn't have been better, and while we were there we could still get home to ride our other horses. Trina stayed with Solo at Waresley, while I commuted back and forth to Perryfields Farm. We had about three girls working at the yard, but we wound things down a bit during the run-up to the Games because I obviously wasn't going to be able to do much competing.

The horses in quarantine couldn't compete anywhere for six weeks, but I don't think that really mattered: they all had plenty of experience. But it was a very long-winded affair. The regulations for travelling to Australia were incredibly strict, and we had to go through everything in fine detail. For example, you weren't allowed to take any wood into the-country, so if you had wooden trees in your boots you had leave the trees behind. The horses' brushes all had to be plastic-backed, not wooden, and everything had to be spotlessly clean. It was all inspected on arrival in Sydney, and if the inspectors thought anything was dirty they burnt it there and then.

It was a huge operation, but even before leaving England I already felt that the new organisational team, with Yogi Breisner in charge, was very different from the one in Atlanta, and we had a great bunch of people on the squad – Scotty, Pippa, Jeanette, Rodney, Mary, Karen and Tina (as travelling reserve). It all had a very different feel to my previous experience four years ago. Yogi had been appointed as our performance manager, a post created by lottery funding, at the beginning of 2000, so he hadn't had long to get to know us all, but he did a terrific job. He worked on the basis that if you, the rider, had done well enough to get selected for the squad then you were likely to be the best judge of what was right for you and your horse. There were more consultations and fewer directives, which we all felt more comfortable with. Here was someone who actually trusted our ability and judgement! Yogi was always available to answer questions and give advice, and over the years he has built up great trust and confidence with the team riders, which I think now would be very hard to beat.

It obviously helped that Yogi had been a very successful competitor in his own right while riding for Sweden in the eighties. He had trained with the famous Swedish trainer, Lars Sederholm, at Waterstock in Oxfordshire, and was already a well-respected trainer himself before he took on the job of managing the British event squad. As far as I am concerned, he is also my sports psychologist because he is the person who talks to me in the ten-minute box just before I set out on the cross-country. He now knows me and my two grey horses so well that he knows exactly what to tell me and what not to tell me, which can be crucial to a rider at that point. His help over the last five years has been invaluable.

When we flew out to Australia we went first to the Gold Coast where the British Olympic Association had their holding camp, and where we were given all our uniform and the other official clothing that we basically had to live in over the next four weeks. We flew down to Sydney the next day, but we didn't stay in the Olympic village because it was so far from the equestrian site. That's why we landed up at the Panthers hotel, which was only about fifteen minutes' drive from Horsely Park, the site of the equestrian Olympics and where the horses were now based, though they were still in quarantine. Yogi was pretty relaxed about our accommodation, and he certainly didn't mind if we had a few drinks and a few late nights – we were three weeks away from the start of the competition, so it wasn't going to do us any harm. Yogi is well aware that eventing is a high-risk sport and that we all need moments of silliness and light-hearted fun to help us relax and forget about our worries. The only drawback was that Matt Straker, our new Performance Director, was an ex-SAS man and an absolute fitness fanatic, and he expected us to go out running every morning. I went on the first day, which was fine, but on the second morning Matt decided that we would do an SAS-style exercise, and took us off on a ten-mile expedition. The following day I was so stiff and sore I could hardly move; I decided that was quite enough fitness training for me.

By the time we got to Sydney I did have some serious worries because Solo hadn't travelled very well on the long flight out and was still sickly. Off the back of that, he suffered a bit of azoturia (muscle cramping), which was not good news for a horse expected to be ready to compete in a three-day event in less than three weeks. I thought, "Here we go again – if they could kick me out of the team for a bruised foot in Atlanta, where do I stand on this one?" It seemed very likely that I would be dropped. I felt that there wasn't really long enough for us to sort out a problem of this kind, and I certainly didn't want to run if it might be detrimental to the horse.

But when I talked to Yogi he was very supportive. He said he had selected me because he wanted me on the team, and that they were going to try to make sure I could stay on it.

Jenny Hall, the team vet, was confident that she could get Solo better and that he would be able to run, which was brilliant to hear. She and Trina sat down and carefully planned his diet, and he was given litres of fluids to flush out his system. We also changed his exercise regime, giving him very little dressage and hardly any trot work. Instead, we took him out onto the gallops and walked him for a while, and then cantered him. The cantering seemed to me a very risky thing to be doing with a horse with muscle problems, but Jenny was incredibly confident and positive about the way she was handling it, so I put my trust in her. We didn't do any dressage training until a week before the Games started. This was so different from Atlanta. In Sydney I felt that everyone was behind me, willing the horse to recover. It gave me so much confidence, and by the time the competition started I was determined to do as well as I possibly could to repay them for what they done for me.

This time it wasn't me who had the hard luck story, it was Rodney Powell. While I was quietly worrying about Solo and assessing my chances of competing in the Games, Rodney hit the headlines by falling off his horse and breaking his ankle. He had been returning from exercising Flintstone when the horse spooked at something, reared up and spun round, and then fell over on top of his leg. Poor Rodney was in hospital for a couple of days and had to have his leg in plaster. He must have felt as miserable as hell, but he's a great guy with an irrepressible sense of humour, and he didn't stay gloomy for long.

Rodney is one of those people who have an incredible zest for life. He is also a kind and generous person, and we have become good friends. We are both very competitive when we are eventing, but I have long given up trying to compete with him when we're drinking, otherwise I have to take the next day off work. As soon as he was discharged from hospital in Sydney he dragged me off to look at some young horses that he was thinking of buying. I wasn't so sure about this plan, because I was the one who had to ride them for him.

It was all very well him standing there on his crutches giving me directions, but I wasn't prepared to take any risks on unfamiliar horses and land up in the same boat as him. "Just stick that fence up another couple of holes," he'd say to the chap selling the horses. "Definitely not," would be my response. "Oh, go on, you'll be fine," Rodney would chirp back.

I have never been more relieved than when I finally cantered into the arena on the first day of the competition in Sydney. It had been such a long wait – three weeks or four years, depending how you chose to look at it. My first attempt to ride for the British team, in Atlanta in 1996, had been thwarted just one day before I had been due to compete, and it had taken me another four years to get back on the squad. Then in Sydney I'd had serious doubts about my chances of competing, and had spent the best part of our three weeks out there living with those doubts. When I finally entered the dressage arena, I felt as if a cloud had lifted. At last, I really was riding for the British team.

Jeanette and I were the first two riders to go for the team, so we had decided not to take part in the parade in the opening ceremony on the previous evening, as we didn't want to get too tired. We knew it would be a very late night (2am or possibly 3am), so we watched it on the television at the house that we had all moved into just before the start of the Games. Missing the ceremony didn't bother me that much because I'd experienced the one in Atlanta, but it was Jeanette's first Olympics so it was a pity for her. She had a bad cold at the time so she was struggling a bit anyway, but she still did a fantastic job the next day as our first rider. It didn't help any of us that the British team was drawn immediately after the Australians, so every time one of us went into the arena to do our dressage we had to cope with noise and applause from the home crowd as they cheered their own rider leaving the arena. Jeanette's horse, Over To You, can be quite tense at the best of times, and she had to follow the Australian Andrew Hoy, who had just done a lovely test on Darien Powers, and was happily acknowledging the uproar that greeted his performance. Everyone was delighted when she still managed to produce one of her best dressage tests on this horse.

We had all experienced the atmosphere in the dressage arena at Badminton; this was much more intense. But Chris Bartle had prepared Solo and me very well beforehand, and we did one of our best ever tests to go into second place behind Andrew Hoy at the end of that first day. Andrew's test had been so good that he was a massive 13.4 penalties ahead of me, but I was still delighted. In retrospect, having to back off the flatwork for two weeks with Solo was probably the best thing for him. He can get a bit fed up with the work anyway, and there is always a temptation to overdo things when you are preparing for something as big as the Olympics.

The next day Pippa and Ian also produced personal bests in the dressage, and Pippa took over second place behind Andrew Hoy, with a much closer score than mine! She and her European Champion partner, Supreme Rock, were only two penalties behind him and our team went into second place behind Australia, with less than three points separating the two teams. USA were lying third at this stage, and that's the way it stayed to the end of the competition. Try as we might, we could not catch up with and overtake the Australians who kept slowly drawing away from us. Their lead of 2.6 penalties after the dressage increased to 12.8 after the cross-country, and ended up at 14.2 after the show jumping. We were always close and we always felt that we were in with a chance, but we couldn't quite get there.

Mike Etherington-Smith, the course designer at Blenheim and Chatsworth, had designed the track in Sydney, which was big, bold and inviting. Jeanette put up another great performance as our pathfinder, coming home clear within the optimum time. Then it was my turn, and I had a fantastic round. My big concern had been the first water complex, where there was quite a decent bounce in, just as there had been at Badminton the previous year when we'd had a stop and I'd fallen off. But since then I had done all that I could to deal with the problem. We'd had some roll top fences built and I'd done plenty of schooling over that sort of thing, going into and through water.

There was downhill approach to the bounce into the first water at Sydney, followed by a corner in the water. Luckily for me, the distance between the bounce into the water and the corner was fairly tight. This suited Solo who, like his brother, tends to be quite slow to move forward after landing into water, and so it is easier to hold him for a slightly shorter stride than to push for a long one. We had no problems at the first water; it was at the second water where things got a bit dicey. Here you had to jump into the water over a log, followed by about three strides to a step up onto a bank and then a bounce straight back into the water over another log. I just remember it all being a bit chaotic, with reins everywhere and the horse twisting and turning, but he was always going, always standing up and moving forward, which was the main thing. It was just a question of us both staying together. Seeing it in slow motion on the video is quite entertaining. Solo twisted over the first fence in and I had to let go of the reins and twist myself the other way to stay on board, and throughout the complex we are both trying to maintain our balance so it all looks very messy. That was definitely our worst moment, and after that we got home safely, clear and within the optimum time, which was a fabulous feeling.

Pippa also went well, so we were level pegging with the Australians at this stage, but then Ian had an unlucky fall with Jaybee at the first water. The horse caught its back legs on the second element of the bounce going in, and wasn't able to get re-balanced and organised for the corner in the water, so he almost straddled it and then he tipped forward into the water on the other side off it. Ian got soaked and had to complete the rest of the course slipping about on a wet saddle, and trying to steer with wet reins. He did well to get back, but sadly the next morning Jaybee wasn't presented for the final horse inspection because he was thought to have damaged a suspensory ligament. However, it wasn't the end for the team, as the rest of us got through the inspection without any trouble.

We were close enough to the Australians on the final day to think that we still had a chance of taking the gold medal from them. Jeanette, Pippa and I were all on good show jumpers, and if we could produce good rounds – and the Australians made mistakes – victory was possible. Unfortunately, we didn't produce the goods. Jeanette only had one fence down but was horrified to find that she had picked up six time penalties. I was then very conscious of the time and probably chivvied Solo along a bit too much, and he had two fences down. Then Pippa also knocked two fences down and got three time penalties, so the gold medal slipped away. The frustrating thing was that the Australians also made a lot of mistakes. Had we jumped as well as we did in Athens four years later we would have won the gold medal in Sydney.

I suppose it was that sense of frustration that was still uppermost in our minds when we faced the press shortly after winning the silver medal. We were interviewed for television as soon as the jumping was over, and we obviously came across as being rather disappointed, which we were, but we got quite a lot of stick for it afterwards. "What's the matter with these riders?" people were saying, "They've just won a silver medal, Britain's first Olympic medal in eventing since 1988, and they all look miserable." I suppose it just hadn't occurred to us that what we had done was a great achievement. We were too busy thinking about the gold medal that had so nearly been ours.

Our achievement did eventually sink in, and we had a great party that night to celebrate (with the exception of Ian because he was competing the next day on Arakai in the individual competition). There was some surprise that Ian was chosen to ride for a second time. I think when Rodney was injured, most people expected Tina Gifford, the travelling reserve, to run in his place, but Ian had a spare horse in Sydney, and so he was given Rodney's place.

Sadly none of our individual riders – Ian, Mary King and Karen Dixon – were well enough placed after the dressage to make it up into the medal positions. The individual title went to America's David O'Connor, the silver to Andrew Hoy and the bronze to Mark Todd. It was great to see Mark winning the bronze, as this was his last international event before retiring from eventing and returning to live in New Zealand. Mark has always been helpful to me. I often used to walk the cross-country course with him at big events and was always glad to get his advice, so I was sorry to see him go.

8

Tarnished Gold

Soon after our return from Sydney there was a huge reception for all the Olympic competitors, trainers and team managers at Buckingham Palace, which was a brilliant occasion. Then in December we were invited to the BBC Sports Personality of the Year awards, where we had dinner and watched the award-giving ceremony. Being surrounded by so many famous sports personalities was an incredible experience, and it was a great evening.

The Sydney Olympics had taken place at the end of September, and because we had had to go out to Australia so early we had missed Burghley that year. Two of the New Zealand team riders, Andrew Nicholson and Mark Todd, decided to stay on in England so that they could ride at Burghley, and they flew out later, with less than two weeks to go before the start of the Games. It seemed to be a worthwhile decision, especially for Andrew, because he won the event on Mr Smiffy, though only after making a dramatic recovery on the cross-country when his horse nearly fell over the second part of the Waterloo rails. Any other rider in that situation would almost certainly have ended up on the ground, but Andrew managed to haul himself back from somewhere between the horse's ears and stay on board.

My brother Graham, who had missed selection for Sydney, was also competing there on a horse called Plantagenet of Rushall, owned by Barry Wookey. He had the fastest cross-country round of the event, but then dropped to tenth place when he had two fences down in the show jumping. Although we weren't there, we followed

Burghley as closely as possible, and I think we were all humbled by Vere Phillipps' incredible performance on Coral Cove. After Polly's death, just over a year ago, Vere decided that the best way he could pay tribute to his wife was to continue competing her talented cross-country horse, Coral Cove, himself. But Vere is a show jumper, and so in the space of year he had to go from competing at Novice level in eventing to riding at his first four-star event. Some people thought he was mad to try, but he was totally focused in his determination to run the horse at Burghley, and to do well when he got there. They finished fourth: a fantastic achievement.

As soon as we got back from Sydney, some of the Olympic rides went to Boekelo, but I decided that was going to be too much of a rush. I took Tadzik and Posey Kopanski's horse, The Hustler, to the two-star at Weston Park, where we came third, and I also had time to run Matt Butler and Shear L'Eau in the Advanced at Witton before taking them both to Pau. Matt Butler won his section, but I had a crash on the cross-country with Stan, which gave us both a bit of a shock. It was once fence from home, where there was a double of rails crossing a lane. The striding was a bit awkward; it was either going be one long stride or two short ones. I'd already been round the course on Matt Butler and he'd got two strides in, and he was a bigger striding horse than Stan, so I was aiming to go for the two strides on Stan as well. I shortened him coming into the fence and then he just fell over it. I'm not quite sure why it happened. I'd obviously shut down the engine a bit to get a quiet stride going into the first part of the double, so that we could fit in the two strides, and perhaps I shut it down too much. Anyway, it was a typical eventing scenario: winning on one horse and falling flat on my face on another.

Pau was to be a step down for Matt Butler after his disappointing performance at Badminton earlier in the year, and for Stan it was his second three-star event – we had already come fifth in Saumur, France, in the spring – so in spite of our splat at Witton, I was looking forward to a good run on both horses. Pau is a lovely event in an attractive part of southern France, near the Pyrenees, and we are always well looked after there. Pippa Funnell and I were the only

1. A promising start. On the beach in Pembrokeshire.

2. The Eardisley Primary School football team (six-a-side), 1976.
Back row, left to right: Willy Bryan, David Goodwin, Tim Lane.
Front row: Graham Wood, me, Mark Whinney.

3. Competing at a Pony Club hunter trial at the age of 12 on my first pony Grey Lace.

4. Riding for the Golden Valley Pony Club team at the age of 14 with Barry.

5. Winning the Reserve Championship with Little Boy Blue at the National Working Hunter Pony Championship at Peterborough in 1982.

6. Little Clearway, the chestnut mare we bought as a three-year old who was ridden by my brother Graham at the Junior European Championships in 1985.

7. My parents, Lawson and Margaret, on a picnic at Rhayader Dam in 2004.

8. Riding Welton Apollo at my first Badminton in 1988.

9. Capitano at Badminton in 1997, when we won the Glentrool Trophy.

10. New Flavour, the horse that took me to my first Olympic Games (Atlanta 1996).

11. Perryfields George, who was sold to Italy.

12. Winning Bramham in 1999 with Shear H2O. In front, left to right, Susan and Jeremy Lawton, and George Lane-Fox.

13. Cruiseway at Badminton in 1998.

15. A long walk back to the stables. Shear H2O at his first Badminton in 1999, after a fall at the lake.

14. What happened next? Shear H2O as an 8 year old competing in Achelschwang. We had a clear round and finished in third place!

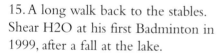

16. Trina competing Air Cruise at Tythrop Park in 1999. The horse won the Athens test trial in 2003 with Terry Boon - a good omen perhaps?

17. First horse inspection, Sydney 2000 with Shear H2O.

19. On our way to the podium to collect our team silver medal in Sydney. Left to right: Ian Stark, Pippa Funnell, Jeanette Brakewell and me.

18. On the cross country in Sydney 2000 with Shear H2O.

20. Matt Butler competing at Pau, France, in 2000.

21. Haig competing at Gatcombe.

22. Prize-giving at Badminton in 2002 with Shear H2O and Brer Rabbit.

23. Brer Rabbit jumping the Hay Wagon at Badminton.

24. Shear H2O at the World Equestrian Games in Jerez, Spain, where the team won bronze medal.

25. My all time favourite horse Shear H2O.

26. Shear L'Eau at the European Championships in Punchestown, 2003. He was the only horse to finish inside the optimum time on the cross country.

27. Kenneth Clawson, show jumping trainer.

28. Tracey Robinson, team dressage trainer.

29. Yogi Breisner, team manager.

30. "No mistakes!" Leaving the dressage arena in Athens with Shear L'Eau.

31. On the cross country in Athens.

32. Cooling off: Shear L'Eau on the cross country in Athens.

33. Shear L'Eau was one of only two event horses in Athens to jump a double clear round in the show jumping.

34. The British team at the medal ceremony in Athens: Jeanette Brakewell, me, Pippa Funnell, William Fox-Pitt and Mary King.

36. Angela (Trina's mother), Trina and Clare (Trina's sister) in Athens.

35. With Susan Lawton in Athens.

37. At home with Shear L'Eau (Stan, his stable name).

38. On the open-top bus parade of Olympic medallists, London, October 18, 2004.

39. Receiving my gold medal from Princess Anne at Buckingham Palace.

40. A proud moment : with Trina after receiving my MBE, February 23, 2005.

two British riders competing that year, and we arrived at the beginning of the week to find that it was pouring with rain, which was miserable. We assumed that as it was raining so hard at that stage it would stop by the weekend, but it was still raining on the Sunday night when we left. I don't think it stopped once during the entire week.

I remember when I was doing my dressage test on Stan it was raining so hard that water was collecting in the rim of my top hat, like rainwater in a gutter, and then cascading over the sides, especially when I tilted my head down! The weather was unbelievable. We never got the chance to dry out and none of us thought the cross-country could possibly go ahead, but to our amazement it did in the end. I set off on the course with Matt Butler early in the day, and he went very well, but the wet ground made me cautious and we got a few time penalties. By the time I came to ride Stan, there had only been one clear round inside the optimum time. Yogi, who had flown over for the event, was in the ten-minute box and told me that the competition was up for grabs. The going was holding up in spite of the appallingly weather, so I had the confidence to set out quite strongly on Stan, and he just cruised round, giving me a fantastic ride.

We could have won Pau that year if we hadn't had two show jumps down the next day. So once again, I had let slip a chance of victory because of an unsatisfactory show jumping result. There had to be a lesson to learn here. Certainly after Sydney we realised that, as a team, we needed to improve our show jumping, because when the scores are close that is the phase in which you ultimately win or lose medals. The work that we subsequently put in on the show jumping was to pay dividends. At the World Championships in Jerez in Spain, and at the Athens Olympics we were able to salvage medals that we hadn't been expected to win because our show jumping had improved.

So one of my New Year's resolutions for 2001 was to do more work on my show jumping. But 2001 was the year that Foot and Mouth hit Britain, which, though inconvenient for us riders, was a disaster for the farmers. We were still based at Perryfields Farm, so the movement of horses was extremely complicated, and there was a lot of disinfecting going on. Every time we went in and out of the place we had to drive through disinfectant and clean our boots, but at least Martin didn't have to slaughter his sheep. My father wasn't so lucky. By now, he and Mum had moved from Cabalva because Revel had more or less given up farming (she had decided that it wasn't going to pay any more) and was leasing out her land. My parents went to run a small hotel/pub called the Maesllwch Arms in Glasbury, and Dad, still pursuing his love of animals, rented some land nearby at Clyro and put his own sheep on it. Eventually they bought their own bungalow with a bit of land attached so he was able to have more sheep, and he must have been looking after about 200 when Foot and Mouth struck. He had to slaughter the whole lot. He was devastated. Foot and Mouth was so brutal in that way. I remember getting a phone call from them when it happened, but there was nothing I could do to help because I wasn't allowed on their land. They had to remain isolated, and if I went to see them I would be putting Martin's stock at risk. It was a horrible time.

They decided not to restock when it was all over. I think Dad had had enough by then. He decided to go into breeding dogs instead – West Highland Whites, and Boxers – which I presume is much easier, though he might not agree. With hindsight it was probably a good thing he didn't go back into sheep. He was 66 and working too hard for his age, and although it's not the way he would have chosen for it to happen, Foot and Mouth did get him out of the sheep business.

When news of the disease broke in February 2001, I was up at Gleneagles doing a lecture/demonstration with Jeanette Brakewell and Kenneth Clawson. Jeanette and I were riding, while Kenneth commented on what we were doing, explaining things and asking us questions. It was quite a good format. We had planned to stay up at Gleneagles that night after the lecture and drive back in the morning, because it's such a long journey – about ten hours. But when we started talking about the implications of the outbreak, we realised that we might be stopped from travelling with the horses the following day, in which case we could be stuck at Gleneagles for months, which would be very expensive! So we packed up after the lecture and set off home at about midnight. We all shared the driving, including Paul Davis, Kenneth's partner, who had been with us at Gleneagles, and we made it home before any restrictions came into force.

What should have been a great year off the back of Sydney 2000 turned out to be a very strange one. Even when the Foot and Mouth outbreak settled down and we eventually got going with the horses, it wasn't a very good year for me. I managed to get Shear L'Eau to Saumur, in France, about the only three-star event that was up and running in the spring, but we'd had very little preparation. He was a bit bright in the dressage and we finished thirteenth. There was no Badminton and no Bramham that year, so Shear H2O was aimed at the European Championships in the autumn. I had thought about taking him to Lexington, the four-star event in America, in the spring, but in the end thought it would be better to give him a rest. The previous year had obviously taken its toll on him, probably more than we realised at the time. In the space of five months he'd come second at Badminton, spent over six weeks away from home, flown around the world, and competed at the Olympic Games, with all the hype, the tension and the pressure that an event of that kind entails.

To make matters worse, he and Trina had had a very difficult journey back from Sydney. One of the engines on the aeroplane had blown up as they took off from the airport at Sydney, so they flew the first leg to Singapore with only three engines working. In Singapore they had to change aircraft, so some fifty horses all had to be unloaded and reloaded. It was incredibly hot, and the whole thing was very stressful.

Shear H2O is a tough horse who always tries his hardest, and he picked himself up and did the Europeans, but I'm not convinced that he was fully recovered from Sydney. You do sometimes get horses that come back from gruelling trips of that kind and never perform quite so well again. Perhaps they just lose heart, and don't want to push themselves to the limit any more. I don't think H2O would ever give up – it's not in his nature – but we had asked a lot of him in 2000.

The European Championships were in Pau and, despite our lack of competition practice because of the Foot and Mouth outbreak, our team still won the gold medal, but this time I didn't perform well and I was the one with the discard score. Yogi and the others are always very supportive to the fourth member who has either messed up or just hasn't achieved a good enough score to be counted, but when you are that person, you don't feel satisfied. In Sydney I had been elated because mine had been the second best score and I felt that I had made a serious contribution to winning the silver medal there. But in Pau I had mixed feelings. It was nice to win the gold medal – and it was fantastic for Pippa to get her second individual title – but I didn't think that I had done my fair share. This was only my second time on the team, and over the years I've learnt to accept that that's what being on a team is all about. The best three scores count so there is always someone whose result isn't included, but everyone plays their part.

Pippa, Jeanette and William Fox-Pit were on the team with me in Pau, and we went in to the lead after the dressage (my score did count at that stage) and stayed there all the way through. Tina Gifford was selected to run as an individual with Captain Christy, and Rodney Powell was supposed to be riding Flintstone, but once again his luck ran out. On the morning we were due to leave for Pau we had a call from Rodney, who was supposed to be travelling with us on our lorry, to say that Flintstone had injured himself. Rodney's place was taken at the last minute by Caroline Pratt, who was a lovely person and great fun to have on the squad. Her death at Burghley three years later was a terrible tragedy.

The cross-country in Pau was quite technical, but it didn't cause too much trouble. My problem came at the first water, where we had a mix-up with the striding. The combination going into the water was probably the most difficult part of the complex as it was made up of three sets of birch rails, the first two on a bounce, followed by a long stride to the third. That actually rode okay, and Shear H2O galloped on through the water to the hanging trough in the middle, after which there was a slight dog-leg to a step, with a bounce to a hedge on the back of it. I had had concerns about the related distance between the trough and the bank, which was a long three strides, but before I set out, as second team member to go, the information coming back was that the horses were getting the three strides easily. So I opted for three strides here and we got three and a half: Solo fell up the bank and couldn't jump the hedge. After that hiccup, I think people wondered why I attempted the fast route at the second water near the end of the course, but I was still trying to get the best possible score that I could at that stage. Being only the second rider on the team, you don't know how things will pan out or what will happen to the two team members after you, so even if you've had a problem you can't just give up. If a lot of people have trouble on the course subsequently, then even with one stop it's possible that your score can still be competitive. Unfortunately, although the reasoning was sound, in practice my plan didn't work. Whether it was because Solo wasn't quite himself or whether it was just another case of getting our striding wrong I'm not sure, but we had a run-out at the jetty as we were coming out of the water.

Yogi and I learnt a lot from that day. Solo is not a forward-going horse in water, which I have always known, but I allowed myself to be persuaded to take three strides to the bank in the first water complex because that's what everyone else was doing, and they were making it look easy. When I'd walked the course, I'd worked out that if I pushed the dog-leg out a bit further and allowed myself a bit more room, there were definitely four strides in it for Solo, which is what would have suited him. But then we watched the first horses on the monitor, including Jeanette on Over To You, who just skipped through the water on three strides. I should have been big enough at the point to say, "No, this is not how my horse does it. I must do this my way." I knew my horse and I should have ridden him in the way that he likes to go.

Luckily the other three members of the team went so well, all of them clear within the optimum time, that my mishaps didn't jeopardise the results. The next day I jumped a clear round in the show jumping, which was satisfying even though it didn't affect the team score. It was nerve-wracking when the others did their show jumping because the French were in second place, only a few penalties behind us, and they were obviously feeling confident on their home territory. Two of their team (which was now reduced to three) jumped clear rounds, putting pressure on William, Jeanette and Pippa, but they all held their nerve – especially Pippa, who was also jumping for the individual title – and each had just one fence down to clinch the team gold medal.

9
Up and Running

Compared to 2001, when the first half of the season never really got off the ground, we were up and running at top speed at the start of 2002. I had two horses, Shear H2O and Brer Rabbit, heading for Badminton, and in the week preceding that I took Shear L'Eau to Lexington, in America, to try his first four-star event. Now that lottery funding was available, a trip to compete in America had become a possibility, and as Lexington is the only other four-star competition available to us in the spring (there were none in Europe), this was ideal for me. I already had two horses to take to Badminton, which is as many as you are allowed to run there, so had I missed Lexington I would have had to wait until Burghley to give Stan his first four-star outing.

The cross-country course at Lexington is designed by Mike Etherington-Smith, and is usually an inviting track, which was why I decided to take Stan there and to take the other two more experienced horses to Badminton. It turned out to be a close-run decision, because that year Lexington suffered from an exceptionally heavy rainstorm, turning the ground from good to bottomless within a couple of hours. It became almost two separate competitions: the first between those that went on the cross-country in the morning, and the second between those who went after the one-hour lunch break. The lunch break was particularly frustrating, because eliminating the break would have been a simple way to improve conditons for those riders who had to go out on the course towards the end of the day.

I was drawn somewhere near the middle of the field and managed to get round the steeplechase without time penalties – I was one of the last people to do this. The ground on the cross-country was just about holding out when we set off, just after lunch, and we had a great round, though unsurprisingly we did get a few time penalties. Unlike Solo, Stan doesn't mind muddy going, so I don't think it was ever going to bother him. He seems to cope with anything, and I was delighted when he finished seventh at his first four-star. William Fox-Pitt and Ian Stark were the only other British riders out in Lexington with me. William came fourth on Stunning, but his second horse, Moon Man, had a late draw and was withdrawn before the cross-country because of bad going, and Ian Stark had a stop on Jaybee.

So then it was back for Badminton. Trina had stayed at home to keep the two Badminton horses working for me while I was away. One of these, Brer Rabbit, had only arrived at our yard the previous winter when his owners, John and Annie Bennett, were looking for someone to ride him. He had had the 2001 season off because of an injury, and his previous rider, Owen Moore, had decided to take a break from eventing. He had already done Burghley in 2000, so he was very experienced, but he was a difficult horse to keep sound because he didn't have the best of feet. He couldn't take the work in the school: his feet just weren't designed to go round in circles. We used to swim him to help get him fit, and he was all right if we galloped him in straight lines, but it was a pity I couldn't do more schooling with him because he was a fabulous cross-country horse. He was a kind soul with a big heart, and very different to ride from Shear H2O because he would pick up the bridle and gallop on the cross-country. He'd just cruise round, and I didn't feel that I had to nudge him forward all the time.

So I had two marvellous horses to ride at Badminton that year. The dressage went reasonably well, though not unexpectedly Brer Rabbit was about halfway down the field after his test. Solo did a good test, but despite our best efforts we were out of the top ten, in fourteenth place, at the end of the first two days. The competition was particularly strong at Badminton in 2002. People like Pippa,

William, Andrew Hoy, Blyth Tait, Rodney Powell and Mary King were all ahead of me after the dressage. But the scores were very close, so I still felt that there was plenty to play for. I've never led from the front in a competition of this level, so I was used to having to make up ground. Hugh Thomas had designed a particularly testing course, which would probably be to my advantage on Solo, who now seemed to be completely back on form. The going was also good, so everything was in our favour; all I needed now was an impressive cross-country performance to put my failings in Pau behind me.

Fortunately this is exactly what I got. My first ride was on Brer Rabbit, whose brilliant round filled me confidence to do the same again, though slightly faster, on Solo. We picked up a couple of time penalties (only four people got back within the optimum-time that day) but our performance was good enough to take us into fifth place. The next day in the show jumping both horses jumped clear again, which was a real bonus, and when Polly Stockton and Andrew Hoy both had fences down, Solo and I moved up to third place behind William Fox-Pitt on Tamarillo, and Pippa Funnell, who won the event on Supreme Rock.

To me, this was almost as good as winning. Although there had been one or two occasions when I had missed my chance to win a big event because of a fence down in the show jumping, I felt that I had reached the top of the sport at a time when it was being dominated by two of the most outstanding riders of recent years. I knew I wasn't quite as talented as them, but if I just kept chipping away, one day I hoped I might come out at the top. Every era throws up its stars. In eventing we'd had Lucinda Green, Ginny Leng and Mark Todd, and now it was the era of Pippa Funnell and William Fox-Pitt. I suppose it was a bit like Richard Johnson coming up against Tony McCoy in racing: he was always going to struggle to beat him. In any other era, Richard would have been a worthy champion National Hunt jockey on numerous occasions. I certainly wasn't complaining about my lot in eventing though, because I had good horses and I was getting on the team, so I was still having a good run in the sport. The last thing I wanted to do was let any frustrations about not winning affect my riding, because my livelihood was at stake – I had a business to run that hinged on my career. But I am a very competitive person and I always put myself under pressure to win, especially at the big events.

Perhaps that was why I entered no fewer than four horses for the CIC three-star international one-day event at Thirlestane in August. This event isn't on a par with Badminton and Burghley, but it does attract a strong entry. Since Mark Todd had retired from the sport at the Sydney Olympics, I had been given the ride on his Olympic horse, Diamond Hall Red, owned by Pat Smith who lived not far from me in Droitwich. This had brought my number of four-star horses up to four, so I thought I had better run them all at Thirlestane. I was hoping to take Stan and Diamond Hall Red to Burghley, and to go to the World Championships with Solo, so these three horses certainly needed an outing at this level, but I don't think I would choose to run four horses in one international class again. It was non-stop action all the way through the cross-country, and I barely had time to draw breath. As soon I'd done a round on one horse, I had to get on and warm up the next, then set off cross-country on that one, come back and warm up the next one. Fortunately, I had four great cross-country rounds, and all the horses were placed. Stan came out on the top, with first place, Solo was sixth, Brer Rabbit was fifteenth and Diamond Hall Red sixteenth. So the long trip to Scotland had been well worth it.

Burghley was next on the agenda, and I was looking forward to giving Stan his first four-star outing in England, and to have a crack at the event on the more experienced Diamond Hall Red, who had won Burghley with Mark on board in 1999. But Diamond Hall Red could be quite excitable in the dressage, and I think it had taken all Mark's talent and skill to produce a good test on him. I didn't know the horse very well and I certainly didn't manage to work Mark's magic on him. We had a fairly disastrous dressage and so I decided to pull him out of the competition and run him at Boekelo instead. It was very disappointing because he was certainly a four-star calibre horse in his jumping ability. He was a lot better in Boekelo, I think because the dressage test at a three-star event is not so demanding and so he probably didn't get so anxious. He cruised around the cross-country there, as I'd expected, and we finished eleventh.

More disappointing than Diamond Hall Red's dressage at Burghley was the fact that I could have won the event on Stan if I hadn't had a show jump down on the final day. He certainly deserved to win it. Wolfgang Feld, a great cross-country course builder, had designed a formidable course at Burghley that year, a real rider-frightener. Although Stan had already jumped a four-star track at Lexington, it had been a rather more inviting course than the one confronting us at Burghley. I thought the most unnerving fence was the Burghley Bank, on the site of the old sunken road near the Trout Hatchery. You had to jump onto the bank and then off again over a big chair fence, and there was huge drop at the back of it. But Stan went brilliantly over that and the rest of the course. Sometimes you have cross-country rounds that are clear, but don't feel particularly good – a bit like my round in Athens – but this one at Burghley felt wonderful: everything was right about it. It had been the horse's biggest challenge of his career, and we had pulled off a class round.

We moved up to third place from our seventh position after the dressage, and when New York, Andrew Nicholson's horse, had to be withdrawn the following morning, we crept up another place. Polly Stockton was in the lead at this stage on Word for Word, another horse previously ridden by Mark Todd, but the top eight riders were all very close. My one fence down, the last on the course, dropped me to fifth place, and Polly Stockton also lost her chance of winning when she lowered a fence, handing first place to William Fox-Pitt on Highland Lad.

I have looked at the video time and time again trying to work what I did wrong. Did I support him too much? Did I use my hands too much to lift him off the floor? I think possibly I did. When you are riding a horse like Stan, who is a good jumper, you do have to look at yourself and think about what you might have done; it's not as if he is just a careless, clumsy oaf. I'm sure it was significant that he hit the last fence – perhaps I got too tense, and tried too hard. Ironically, it was a dog-leg turn to the final fence, just as it was in

Athens two years later, which is why, at those Olympics, I simply couldn't allow myself to make the same mistake again.

I was bitterly disappointed. You don't get many chances to win a four-star event and I'd just blown one of them. I felt sorry for myself, and for the owner Jeremy Lawton, who was still waiting patiently for me to win a major event. But there wasn't too much time to mull over what might have been: next stop was Jerez for the World Equestrian Games, when seven equestrian disciplines – eventing, pure dressage, show jumping, carriage driving, endurance riding, vaulting and western riding – hold their world championships at the same venue within the space of twelve days. It is a huge occasion for the equestrian calendar. In Jerez, there were over 300 horses taking part in the competitions, and 52 nations involved. There were certainly a lot of horses squeezed into a small space (basically in the middle of the town) so we did feel quite confined. But we were well looked after, and the organisers put on a fantastic display for the opening ceremony.

Britain's eventing team had started as one of the favourites in Jerez. We had the same four riders on the team as we'd had in Pau, except that this time William had Tamarillo, the horse he'd finished second on at Badminton in the spring. The horses had flown out to Spain, rather than being driven, and Solo was well after the flight, which was a huge relief. It was very hot all the time, and with such a restricted area to exercise the horses, I was glad that we arrived only three days before the event started, so we weren't stuck there for too long. The cross-country course was outside Jerez, about half an hour's drive away, which was a new experience for me. It meant that you couldn't just go and walk the course when you felt like it, you had to fit in with everybody else, and once the competition had started it was difficult to find a time when there wasn't somebody doing their dressage. We'd end up going out to the course very early in the morning before the competition started, or late in the evening when everyone had finished.

Normally, I like to walk a course three or four times, depending whether or not I have any particular concerns about certain fences or combinations. The initial course walk, which I usually do with other team members, is just to get a general feel of the track, to see what's there and get an idea of how it will ride. On the second walk, which I nearly always do on my own, I work out exactly what my lines will be between the fences and coming into them, and where I want to jump each fence. I usually do my third walk with Yogi so he knows what I am planning to do, and I can also get advice from him. I might walk it again after that, or just go back and look at specific fences.

Mike Tucker had designed a serious championship course in Jerez. It was a big, twisty track, with a lot of fences coming off the turn, so that you were constantly chopping and changing direction, and it was difficult to get the horses flowing and into a rhythm. The course had been built completely from scratch on rocky terrain, so they'd had to bring in enormous amounts of topsoil and plant new grass. They had done a fantastic job and it all looked wonderful, but you couldn't get away from the fact that there was rock four inches underneath the soil, which made the going very jarring for the horses. Almost £2 million had been spent building the course, which set a few alarm bells ringing, because eventing was still under scrutiny by the International Olympic Committee for being too expensive to run as an Olympic sport. HRH the Infanta Dona Pilar de Borbon, President of the FEI, made her feelings known about the excessive costs at a press conference during the Games and there was a big hullabaloo about it all.

As soon as I saw the first water complex, with the long, sloping bank going into the water, I knew I wouldn't want to attempt the quick route with Solo. The bank was like a slide, so you couldn't be sure when your horse would take off from it to jump into the water, and yet within three strides of landing in the water there was an island complex to negotiate. There was too much left to chance, and not enough to skill and riding ability, and I just didn't want to take the risk. Once again, I was second to go on the team, and Yogi was quite happy with my decision about the water complex. Jeanette, our pathfinder again, had decided to take the fast route here, and did it successfully, coming back with another clear round (her fourth successive team clear on Over To You).

I stuck to my decision and went the long route at the water, which was a bit of a fiddle because you had to go through a tunnel under the bank then jump a fence in the water, and then go all the way round the island to jump another fence. Anyway, we successfully negotiated that and went on to complete what I thought was a clear round, and I was feeling reasonably pleased about it all until I heard the results for my round on the loudspeaker. Twenty jumping penalties – how could that be? Then Yogi said that he thought I had circled between the A and B elements of an obstacle. There was a complex of three huts, and the first two of these were numbered A and B, which means that they have to be treated as a single obstacle and you cannot circle between them. The third hut was numbered separately, so I could have circled in front of that. When Solo landed over the first hut, I thought he had gone lame: his action didn't seem quite right (he had in fact lost a front shoe, though I didn't know that at the time). So I trotted him for a couple of strides, and then he seemed okay so I carried on, but that momentary lapse of concentration on the obstacles was fatal. Before I knew it, I'd turned a circle in order to line up for the second hut, and I didn't even realise what I'd done until I heard the scores.

It was the most awful moment. The horse had done everything I asked and had completed what turned out to be one of the most difficult championship courses in recent times – there were 25 falls on the course, and only fifty out of the eighty competitors completed it. Solo had, in effect, jumped a clear round, except that the pillock on top had given him twenty jumping penalties. I'd played safe at the first water, only to go and make a hash of it at a relatively straightforward obstacle. It took me a long time to forgive myself for that mistake. I suppose there was a slight excuse in that I was distracted by my concern about the way Solo landed from the first hut, but you have to be sharper than that. It was my responsibility and I had messed up, and this time the team really needed a clear round from me because Pippa and William both ran into trouble at the first water complex. Pippa came down the bank in a very controlled manner on Supreme Rock, but he stumbled and floundered in the water. Then William came down quite quickly on Tamarillo, who is a sharp horse, but he also had problems in the water. So what was the right way to ride this fence? They both picked up twenty penalties here, and suddenly the favourites for the team medal were looking a bit out of it.

We all felt pretty miserable that evening. We'd started the day off in the lead, and now we were in fourth place, nearly sixteen penalties behind France, so a team medal looked unlikely. In fact Yogi was more concerned at this stage that we didn't drop down to fifth place, below New Zealand, which was only 6.8 penalties behind us. If we did that, we would fail to qualify for the next Olympic Games. It all looked a bit grim, but we knew that as a team we were now quite good at the show jumping, as we had proved in Pau the previous year. The only thing we could do was to go out the next day and jump to the best of our ability, and hope that other people would make a lot of mistakes.

I had one fence down on Solo, and so, as in Pau, my score was the discard, though not by much this time. William then jumped a clear round on Tamarillo, which raised our hopes, particularly as there seemed to be poles flying in all directions. Pippa had only one fence down, but the French weren't giving much away and our chances of overtaking them didn't look good. Then came the biggest surprise. Stuart Tinney, Australia's best placed team rider had six fences down, and suddenly Australia, which looked to have had the silver in the bag, was in trouble. It meant that if Jeanette, who had been lying in sixth place individually after the cross-country, could jump round with no more than one fence down and with no time penalties, we could just slip ahead of Australia and take the bronze medal behind France and the USA. Jeanette was brilliant under the pressure and jumped to order, so that we moved into the bronze medal position by just 0.4 penalties. This was an unexpected bonus, but there was more to come for Jeanette.

To be honest, you don't go into the show jumping on the final day in sixth place, have a fence down, and then hope to win an individual medal. But to our amazement the fences kept coming dowri, and Jeanette edged her way up the score-board until she reached the silver medal position, which was a great result for her.

So although overall it was a disappointing World Championship for the team, considering we had started out as favourites, we did at least manage to salvage a couple of medals and qualify for the Olympics.

10

In the Frame

It had certainly crossed my mind that two disappointing performances in two consecutive years for the British team wouldn't do much for my prospects of selection for the 2003 European Championships, due to take place in Punchestown, Ireland, in the autumn. All I could now was to push ahead with the next spring season, try to stay in the frame and get good enough results to convince the selectors that I could still be an asset to the team. I still had four horses at four-star level, so I decided to take Shear L'Eau back to Lexington again, along with Diamond Hall Red. The other two, Shear H2O and Brer Rabbit, could run at Badminton the following week.

Trina didn't come to Lexington because she needed to look after the two Badminton horses and keep them in work for me, so Paul Davis came out to help. He flew over with the horses and with a list of instructions as long as his arm. I've got so used to having Trina with me at the big events and, as I don't get involved much with her side of things, I don't have a clue what to do when she's not there. So she sent Paul out with lists of which boots each horse had for working in, which boots they had for cross-country, which boots for show jumping, which bridles they wore for working in and which for competing. There were instructions about which studs to use, what to feed the horses, how to look after them after the cross-country, and so on. It was mind-boggling. Paul and I had endless discussions about what we should be doing. One day, having consulted the list, we couldn't agree on which bridle I was supposed to be using. I was sure I had the right one, but he was convinced it should be a different one. There was a lot of bantering, and in the end we decided we'd have to ring up Trina to sort it out.

Paul is a wonderful character, quick witted and very entertaining. He'd spent a year looking after the great show jumper Milton when John Whitaker was competing with him, so he knew what he was doing. On the morning of Stan's dressage, he was plaiting his mane with white elastics when Lucinda Green, one of the selectors, peered over the stable door and asked him why he wasn't using a needle and thread. "Move with the times, darling, move with the times!" was his immediate reply.

Logistically, the trip to Lexington is a tough fortnight, especially with two horses, and Paul did a superb job. The horses flew out to New York about a week before the event started, and then spent two days in quarantine before being driven overnight to Lexington, which takes at least twelve hours. They arrived on Saturday morning, having spent the last three days standing on an aeroplane, in a stable, or on a truck. If you had to leave a horse standing in your stable at home for three or four days just before a three-day event you'd be pulling your hair out, but because you have to do it to get to Lexington, you just do. It's not ideal for a fit horse to be kept immobile for so long, but they seem to cope. On the Saturday they got taken out to eat a bit of grass and have a walk around, and on Sunday it was much the same routine. I arrived on the Sunday night, so I hacked the horses out on Monday, did some work with them on Tuesday, and then the trot up was on Wednesday. Once the competition was over, Paul had to stay on for a couple more days with the horses and then fly back with them.

There were quite a few British riders at Lexington in 2003, and we pretty well swept the board. Pippa won the event on Primmore's Pride, Polly Stockton was second, and William Fox-Pitt third. Buck Davidson, the only American to finish in the top five, was fourth, and I came fifth on Stan. (I still hadn't managed to do a very good dressage test on Diamond Hall Red, but he went brilliantly on the cross-country to finish in fourteenth place). So we felt we'd got our own back on the Americans after their success in winning the team gold medal at the World Equestrian Games in Jerez the previous year. William stirred things up even more by making some comment about us beating the Americans on our second-string horses, just to annoy Mark Phillips, the US team manager. We were certainly feeling quite pleased with ourselves as we headed back to England to compete at Badminton.

While I was in Lexington, Trina had called to tell me that the bid we had put in on a house at Naunton, near Worcester, had been successful. We were about to become the proud owners of a disused and very run-down old dairy farm. We had been looking for a place of our own for nearly a year, and Trina had spotted this farm in early March, but when I first saw it I didn't think it would be any good for us. There just didn't seem to be much there, and certainly no stables or fenced fields: just a tiny house, a milking parlour, a barn and a bit of land. But she had convinced me that it had potential. We'd had to put in a sealed bid for the property, so it was very exciting when we found out that we'd got it. The only problem was that we didn't have the money available at that point to pay for the place, so I was panicking about where the cash was going to come from. Winning Lexington would have helped! Luckily we had a very good solicitor who managed to keep stalling the local council, which was the vendor and didn't seem to be in that much of a hurry in any case. In the end we didn't exchange contracts until November, by which time we had managed to sort out the finances.

Badminton was another good event for me. I had two fabulous cross-country rounds, both within the optimum time. Luckily I had an early draw on Shear H2O, so we were out on the course before the rain set in, though it was already slippery in places. Solo gave me a bit of worry at the lake when he managed to fiddle in a small stride between the two big logs into the water, where there was supposed to be just a bounce, but otherwise it was a good round. By the time I rode Brer Rabbit, the conditions had deteriorated rapidly, and one fence, the Charisma Puzzle, had started to cause a lot of trouble. The obstacle consisted of a large, open ditch with a bounce to a big brush fence, followed by a narrow brush fence on the turn. The ground either side of the open ditch had become so muddy that there was no clear dividing line between the ditch and the landing and horses were having trouble seeing the ditch itself: some put their feet straight in it. There were quite a few falls here, so the Ground Jury decided to remove the fence from the course with only about eleven horses still to run, adjusting everyone's time accordingly.

So Brer Rabbit didn't have to do that fence, though I think he would have managed it if he had. He gave me a great ride despite the mud, and I think he got round that day by sheer guts and determination – another horse with a big heart. I had found it increasingly difficult to get him fit because of his bad feet, and most of his work had been done in the swimming pool, which meant an awful lot of swimming to get him ready for this level of competition. Without the time spent on his flatwork we were never going to be able to be very competitive, and we were placed 43rd after the dressage, but his cross-country was so good that we moved up to a final eighteenth place. Solo copied his brother, and gave me another fifth place at a four-star event, after knocking down one show jump, but we couldn't have done better than fourth even if we had jumped clear. Pippa Funnell, on Supreme Rock, had been well out in front after the cross-country, and had two fences in hand for the show jumping, but she had everyone on tenterhooks on the last day because she went slowly and carefully and collected six time penalties, nearly giving away her first place to Pia Pantsu, the first Finnish rider to complete Badminton. After her win, the talk was all about whether she could win Burghley as well, and claim the 250,000 US dollars that Rolex was offering to any rider who could win the three top events – Lexington, Badminton and Burghley – in succession. I honestly don't think anyone, least of all Rolex, imagined that it would ever happen.

I hadn't taken Matt Butler to Badminton this time because we had decided only to run him in one-day events. He'd done Badminton twice, and both times had had trouble on the cross-country, and we felt that he didn't cope happily with four-star courses. Instead, I took him to the international one-day event at Chatsworth the week after Badminton. I was quite worried about our prospects when I saw the cross-country course there because it was very technical, with a lot of narrow fences and arrowheads. Matt Butler tends to be a bit wicked at narrow fences, and often has his eye on the escape route instead of the fence, but for some reason this time he seemed to want to do it, and he stormed round the course. We had quite a lot of time faults because he gets a bit strong and so I have to waste time setting him up, but with a clear round in the show jumping, we finished in fifth place. I was absolutely delighted for his owner, Diana Fitzroy, because she hadn't had the best of luck with her horses. She'd been a part owner of New Flavour and had travelled all the way out to Atlanta, only to see him withdrawn from the competition on the day of the first horse inspection, and Matt Butler didn't turn out to be the four-star horse that we had hoped for. Diana has always been a very loyal and supportive owner, and is passionate about her horses, so this success at Chatsworth meant a lot to her.

Rodney Day, who I had met through Roddy Dean in Ireland, had moved back to England the previous year, bringing a string of horses with him. He'd asked me to take on the ride of these horses, so in the spring I had a yard full of "Fox" horses. There was Fox on the Run and V.A. Fox, who both went to Bramham with me; Fox Himself, Flying Fox, Rocco Fox, Quick Brown Fox, Fandango Fox and Arctic Fox Too. I competed them all, and we gradually sold them on. Fox on the Run, a New Zealand thoroughbred who is a good galloper and jumper, was sold to a young British rider, and the only one we have kept is Arctic Fox Too, a very nice horse who did the two-star three-day event at Weston Park in 2004.

As far as my team selection prospects were concerned, the two greys had come up trumps when it mattered, giving me good results at Badminton and Lexington, so now they were both being considered by the selectors for the European Championships. It was nice to have two options. I had a lot of discussions with Yogi about which of the two horses might be the best choice for Punchestown. My feeling was that Stan had always had the potential to be better than Solo, but it isn't always potential that wins competitions. Solo may be slightly less talented, but he is a formidable competition horse: he nearly always gets good results. But Stan had now got plenty of experience at four-star level, and was getting more consistent, so I think the feeling amongst the selectors was that it was time to give him a try on the team. It was obviously better to ride him first at the Europeans, rather than wait for a year and then try him out for the first time at the Olympics.

Stan won the World Cup qualifier at Lulworth Castle in July, and then I took the two brothers to Gatcombe for the Open Championships. With the help that I'd been getting from Tracie Robinson, Stan's dressage was continuing to improve and he did a better test than Solo. They copied each other in the show jumping by having one fence down, but Stan came off the cross-country one second faster than his brother to finish fourth, while Solo was eighth. Stan, now eleven, was beginning to turn the tables on his thirteen-year-old brother. Both horses are very fast across country because they don't pull, so I can just keep riding them forward, but at Gatcombe it is very difficult to achieve the optimum time because of the terrain there. It is a real skill to be able to go quickly without running out of petrol, and to keep your horse balanced and jumping happily over the steep hills and undulations. In spite of the fact that I have to gallop past the place where Capitano died, Gatcombe is one of my favourite events, because it is such a challenging track and I have had some great cross-country rounds there.

So it was Shear L'Eau who got the nod from the selectors for Punchestown, and I was very excited about his prospects there. Jeremy Lawton was more nervous than excited: the last time he'd been to Punchestown was six years ago when Shear H2O and I had fallen twice at the water, but he hates to miss an event. He had been very disappointed when he couldn't get out to Lexington in 2002, when I took Stan there for the first time. It nearly killed him not to be able to watch what was happening. Luckily my mobile phone didn't work in America, but Yogi's did, so he was the one to get all the calls from Jeremy, who couldn't bear not to know how things were going. Jeremy is a great owner though, because he never interferes at events and gives me plenty of space and time to myself when I need it. I think he gets more nervous than I do when it comes to the cross-country.

Fortunately for Jeremy's nerves and for my place on the British team we had a successful trip to Punchestown this time. The Irish always put on a good event there, and for the European Championships there was a great atmosphere, though we were quite glad to be staying in a smart hotel this time rather than in our horseboxes on the event site. The British team – Pippa, William, Jeanette and I – was exactly as it had been in Jerez the previous year, except that Pippa had Walk on Star and William had Moon Man because Supreme Rock and Tamarillo were both out with temporary injuries. Mary King and Tina Cook were the individuals. Most of us were exhausted by the time we got to Punchestown because we'd had horses running at both Burghley and Blenheim three-day events during the previous two weeks, so this was our third week away from home. I had taken Solo and V.A. Fox to Burghley, and Fox on the Run and Another Garrison to Blenheim.

At Burghley, the cross-country hadn't been very much different from the previous year, but it seemed to cause a lot of unexpected problems. It was clearly too much of a challenge for V.A. Fox, who put in two refusals at the Flowerbeds on the Waterloo Hills, another stop at the Pig Sties and a fourth stop at Capability's Cutting, where we were eliminated. It is a long walk back to the stables from there. Solo had done a slightly disappointing dressage and we were thirteenth at that stage. We then collected six time faults on the cross-country and had one fence down in the show jumping to finish eleventh, so it wasn't a great Burghley for me. Anyway, all eyes were focused on Pippa Funnell and Zara Phillips that year. It was Zara's first four-star competition, so there was a lot of media interest in her, and it was Pippa's chance to win the Rolex Grand Slam. Zara had gone into the lead after an impressive cross-country round on Toy Town, so she was last into the show jumping, following Pippa who had just gone clear on Primmore's Pride and had left her no margin for error. Zara's one fence down gave Pippa her 250,000 US dollar award, a Rolex watch and a blaze of publicity. It was fantastic for her, and truly deserved; and it was also tremendous for the sport because her Grand Slam win was on the front pages of the newspapers the next morning.

I think the interest that Pippa created in the sport that weekend at Burghley carried through to Punchestown, and there was certainly a sense that eventing in Britain was on the crest of a wave. British riders had dominated the Burghley results and now we were at the European Championships hoping to bring back a team medal – preferably gold – and of course there was media interest in Pippa again because she was defending her two previous European titles. Our first impression of the cross-country course was that it was a big, demanding track, but I quite liked it. Tommy Brennan designs very imaginative courses, and he had certainly come up with some interesting ideas this time. The one that concerned me was called the Powerscourt Waterfall where there seemed to be water everywhere. You came up three big steps, which was quite an effort for the horses, then there was a sharp right turn to a wall at the top of a very steep slope and either side of the slope were two long, horizontal, wooden structures with water shooting out of them and cascading down the hill. The horses had to jump down through the middle of all this, and at the bottom of the hill there was a hanging beam over water. I thought the whole thing would be quite an eyeful for Stan.

There were so many obstacles involving water – six of them altogether – that Pippa commented that Tommy Brennan must have been a duck in his former life. In fact, Tommy can't swim, and at the 1968 Olympics in Mexico he nearly drowned at the notorious open water jump, where the depth of the water had risen to over a metre and the flooding was so bad that it was almost impossible to know when to take off. Apparently he survived by hanging on to his horse's tail. As soon as I saw the last water complex on his course in Punchestown, where the quickest route was to go through a tunnel to a big drop into the water, with three strides to a bank and bounce over a narrow house-shaped fence, I knew it wasn't for me. Like the water complex at Jerez the previous year, there was too much left to chance. You couldn't predict how far out into the water the horses would land from the big drop, and yet you then had to ride a related distance to the bounce, so it all seemed too big a risk. One of the alternatives was to ride down beside the tunnel and jump some rails into the water, and then ride a dog-leg on four strides to the bounce.

I thought that this would probably only take a couple of seconds longer – if that – because I wouldn't have to spend much time setting the horse up for it; and at least I knew how he was likely to land in the water.

During the summer, Yogi and I had discussed the possibility of me going out first for the team, instead of Jeanette. It was something that Yogi was keen to try, because he felt, probably quite rightly, that I did my best cross-country rounds when I went early in the day. This is because I ride the course exactly as I have walked it and don't get distracted by what other people have done. When I came second at Badminton with Solo in 2000, we were the first out on the cross-country, so I had to stick to my original plans. Jeanette didn't seem to mind swapping places with me, so it was agreed at Punchestown that I would be the trailblazer, and as the British team was drawn sixth out of the eight nations, I was number six on the course. Stan had done a good dressage test on the first day, and we were lying in twelfth place individually and first place with the team, at the start of the cross-country.

Luckily, when I set out on the course I was blissfully unaware of the havoc that had preceded me. The first two competitors, the Italian Fabio Fani Ciotti and the Swedish rider Magnus Gallerdal, had both had falls, and two others had had refusals. Only the Irish rider, Susan Short, had gone clear, and she had picked up sixteen time penalties. Oblivious to all this, I had a fantastic round on Stan, with only one slightly worrying moment when he slipped on top of the Newgrange Mound, a big bank four fences from the start, and we had to put in an extra stride before the narrow fence that followed. It had already started to rain, and it was a murky, wet, grey day; the ground was slippery in places, and with all the banks and undulations it was quite a tough track for the horses. But Stan took it all in his stride, including my route through the last water complex, and we came home clear exactly on the optimum time. I was absolutely delighted, but little did I know at that point that mine would be the only round of the entire day without time penalties.

Poor Jeanette, going in my usual slot of second place for the team, had a disaster at the last water complex, where she had attempted the tunnel route with the big drop. Over To You did the first part all right, but then he got in a bit close to the bank in the water, and fell going up onto it. His fall meant that Jeanette was eliminated, which was a shock for the rest of us, as we had all come to rely on Jeanette going clear. It was the first mistake the horse had made in five consecutive years for the British team, and Jeanette was obviously very upset. I don't think she'll ever want to relinquish her trailblazer spot again. After that, the team orders were to take the long route at the final water complex, so Pippa and William both had to go right round the island in the middle of water, which took ages. They weren't even allowed to attempt the dog-leg that I'd done. Having lost Jeanette's score, I don't think Yogi wanted to take any chances, and the way things were panning out (there was quite a lot of trouble on the course), it was obviously the most sensible thing to do.

William had a near-disaster at the hanging log over the water, and nearly fell flat on his face when Moors Man stepped on his over-reach boot as he landed. How he stayed on board, I don't know, but in one awful second we saw Britain's medal hopes lost and retrieved. Both William and Pippa got time faults, which wasn't surprising given that they had had to take the long route at the last water, but they were clear, so in spite of Jeanette's uncharacteristic fall, we managed to retain our lead over the French. I had moved up to fourth place individually, Pippa was fifth, Mary (as an individual) was seventh with King Solomon, and William was eighth. We only had four fences in hand over the French, so things were a bit tense on the final day, especially when William had two fences down on Moon Man, but then Pippa jumped clear, which took the pressure off me slightly.

I had just one fence down on Stan, which secured the team gold medal, so everyone was delighted, but it ruined my chances of winning an individual medal. When the Belgian rider, Karin Donckers, who had been lying third, had two fences down, I could have moved into the bronze position and won my first individual medal, but instead it was Pippa who took the bronze, and I was fourth. Once again, I had missed my chance because of a single rail down in the show jumping. So it was a day of mixed emotions:

obviously it was fantastic to get another European team gold medal, but it was galling to miss an individual award. The individual gold went to the Frenchman, Nicolas Touzaint, who had led from the start on the impressive nine-year-old Galan de Sauvagère, and who was already being tipped by many as the next Olympic champion.

On November 7th we exchanged contracts on Green Street Farm and we spent the winter working on the place before we could move in. Trina, together with family and friends, did most of the work. I used to spend the mornings at Perryfields Farm, about half an hour's drive away at Inkberrow, riding the horses, and then get over to Naunton at around lunchtime to see how everyone was getting on. Initially, there was a huge amount of clearing to do. Then we put a concrete floor in the old barn so that we could convert it to stables, and we turned the milking parlour into a washroom for the horses and a tack room. We had builders putting in block walls in the old barn, people laying out the all-weather arena, and digging up and laying out the driveway.

We also had another, bigger barn built to create enough stables, but when we got the quote for concreting the floor we decided it was too expensive and that we would do it ourselves. That was a day I would like to forget. Trina and her sister Clare, and Derek Philpot and his son, who are friends of Trina's family, were in charge of the job, which was a lot more complicated than I thought it was going to be. Trying to get the levels right was a nightmare, and they worked from dawn until dusk to get the work completed. I wasn't any use to them at all, so I just made cups of tea and tried to give them moral support, or keep out of the way – whichever seemed to be the most appropriate thing at the time.

We managed to get the horses moved into their new stables a week before our first event, which was quite something. The stables were just finished, but we still had no turnout and no accommodation for the grooms. We had about twenty horses to move, so I just went back and forth with the horsebox until we'd got them all there. By then the house had its kitchen fitted, a bedroom almost finished (minus the carpet) and a bathroom, so we could live in it. Trina, Clare and Tim (Trina's brother), whose wife Karina had just had their first child, continued to work hard on the place, mostly on the stables, fencing and other outside jobs, while I was allowed to concentrate on the horses. My parents came down to help us, and Trina's family were fantastic. They spent a lot of time during the year chipping away at various jobs and getting things done, while I carried on riding and competing. We couldn't have taken on a massive project like this at such an important time in my career if we hadn't had so much help and support from everyone.

11
On Course for Athens

After our success in Punchestown, I knew that Stan (Shear L'Eau) was more likely to be selected for Athens than Solo (Shear H20), but they had both come back into work early in the New Year, before we moved to Naunton. The plan was to aim Solo at Badminton, but to do just a couple of one-day events with Stan, and then give him a break before building up to Athens. The selectors had told me that it wasn't necessary for him to go Badminton, so the choice was mine. If he had been my only four-star horse I'd have been tempted to take him, because I hate missing Badminton: it's still the event we all want to win. There is also a danger that other riders will give such an impressive performance there that the selectors decide they don't need you on the team after all. This happened in 2000 when some of the long-listed riders were told that they didn't need to do Badminton, but then Mary King won it, I came second and Rodney Powell was third, and we all got to go to Sydney. So although Stan had nothing to prove, it didn't mean that I was automatically going to be selected for Athens. In fact Mary King, who had also been told that King Solomon didn't need to run at Badminton, was initially left off the team. It was a calculated gamble: don't run and someone else might take your place, or run and risk injuring your horse.

Although the selectors were happy for Stan to miss Badminton, they did want him to compete at the three-star CIC in Fontainebleau, France, in early March. They were keen to see him do a dressage test somewhere where there was quite a lively atmosphere, so Fontainebleau was chosen because the dressage arena is in the main ring of the show ground, and there are usually plenty of people watching. I decided that we might as well take Solo there as well, so we had to start getting both horses fit early in the year to be ready for the event. Once I had got Stan back into work, Tracie Robinson began helping me. The dressage was still his weakest phase, though with Tracie's help it had been gradually improving, and we had agreed that it would be better to start work on him during the winter rather than wait until the competition season had begun. Tracie had taken over as our official team trainer in 2001, after Chris Bartle had been asked to train the Germans, which at the time had been quite a blow for our own team. Chris had been an inspiration and had taught me an enormous amount, so when he went there was a bit of a gap in my dressage training.

Tracie was trained at the Talland School of Equitation with Pammy Sivewright (now Hutton), and has worked at Dr Bechtolsheimer's yard, where she helped Carl Hester. She has also schooled horses for Mark Todd. When she got involved with our team training I found that I liked her methods and could understand what she was trying to achieve, so I asked if she could teach me on a one-to-one basis. That worked well: not only did she help me enormously but also, as team trainer, she was there to hold my hand at the championships! She is an incredibly enthusiastic trainer. Her support is always 100 per cent and you know she's hurting as much as you are when you don't do well. Tracie had decided that she was going to get Stan working correctly by the Olympics, but to achieve this we had to go step by step, which was sometimes quite frustrating for me as the competitor, because I'd want it all to be perfect there and then. Stan has always been slightly reluctant to take the contact, so Tracie spent a long time working him low and deep until the contact was better established. She has much more patience that me, and she was determined that we would get the basics right before we did anything else.

It seemed to pay off. At his first event, Tweseldown, where we did the Open Intermediate class, he came out and did a good test. Normally at his first "party" of the season he would be a bit sharp, so the fact that he came out focused and into the contact was a relief

– all that hard slog through January and February had done some good. We had a very comfortable run there, finishing second to the German rider, Bettina Hoy, and I was also sixth on Solo. So far it was all going according to plan.

Two weeks later we set off with the two grey boys on my first ever visit to the CIC three-star event in Fontainebleau, but the trip turned out to be almost a complete waste of time. The plan had been for Stan to do a dressage test in a lively atmosphere, but although I had requested that he should be my second ride, they put me about fifth to go on him, which meant that I did my test early on the Thursday morning when there was no one around to watch – not even a British team selector! We did a reasonable rather than a brilliant test, but there was no atmosphere, it was freezing cold and I was feeling very frustrated. Steve and Sharon Green (members of Stan's syndicate), and Jeremy and Susan Lawton had come over to France specially to watch us and it had all got off to a bad start. I was annoyed because I'd requested that the horse be my second ride but, because of the draw, the aim of the exercise was completely unfulfilled. I might just as well have gone to Solihull to do some dressage.

At least Solo, who'd got the later slot, did quite a good test, and the show jumping was worth doing. It was a decent-sized, well-designed course on slightly undulating ground. Stan had two fences down, which made me realise that we still had some work to do in that department as well. It sharpened us both up a bit, so it was a good exercise. Initially, I felt reasonably enthusiastic about the cross-country. It was a well-built course with plenty of challenges – bounces into water, arrowheads, and corners – everything you could want for a good practice round. But when I walked the course again late on Saturday afternoon, after the horses in the earlier competition had already been round it, I found the going in the wood had become very deep. The ground was firm outside, but there was loose, deep sand in the woods, and a sudden change of going can often create tendon trouble.

It was difficult to know what to do. My instinct was to pull out, especially as I hadn't done a particularly good dressage and I'd had two show jumps down, but the owners were there and the selectors had asked me to run. Yogi had now arrived in Fontainebleau. I talked to him about it for quite a long time, and in end I took the bull by the horns and decided I wasn't running either of the horses. Jeremy was fantastic about it and Yogi was very supportive, but I was a bit despondent that my "team selection" run hadn't happened, especially as we'd spent the best part of the week getting to this event. Looking back, I'm glad I took the decision I did. You have to run for the right reasons, and there were a lot of factors that weren't right – one of them being my frame of mind.

By now my schedule had gone slightly awry. Stan should have come back from Fontainebleau for a rest, but I thought we ought to do something other than just the Open Intermediate at Tweseldown, to prove our form. So I spoke to Alec Lochore, the organiser of Burnham Market, and managed to get both horses entered in the special Advanced section that they were running for horses going to Badminton. This section did its dressage in the main arena, which turned out to be an ideal practice because we had to work the horses in well away from the arena, and then walk them over to the main ring just before their test. This is what normally happens at the major competitions: the warming-up area will be some distance from the dressage arena, and horses have to cope with moving from one place to the other without getting uptight or excited about it. There was much more atmosphere at Burnham Market than there had been for Stan at Fontainebleau. Both horses did good tests, with Stan scoring 29.6 and Solo 31.9, and they also both jumped clear over a big show jumping track. I had two great rides on the cross-country – the horses both seemed well within themselves and they made the course feel easy. Stan won the section and Solo was third, *and* there was a selector there to watch. So we finally achieved our objective – producing a good test in a buzzy atmosphere and having a confident run across country – and we had done it by going to an event that took us only three and a half hours to reach, instead of thirteen and a half.

Mandy Stibbe, the selector who watched me at Burnham Market, has had a significant influence on my eventing career. As Chairman of Selectors in 2000, it was Mandy who gave me my first chance to compete on the British team in Sydney. She put her faith in me, which gave me a lot of confidence, and she was very supportive and open with everybody. She and Yogi, the team manager, were part of the new regime established in eventing at the end of 1999, and they had obviously built up a rapport, which had a good influence on us. When you know that the people managing you are all pulling in the same direction, it makes the whole atmosphere so much better.

They brought in the policy of announcing the team for each year's forthcoming championship well in advance, which was a great improvement because it allowed riders to know whether or not they should be preparing for a particular competition. When the team selection was left up until the last possible moment, riders would be running their horses to keep proving them right up until the team was announced. Mandy has put an enormous amount of her time into the sport since the days when she was competing at the top level. When she takes on a job she likes to give it everything. She is still on the Selection Committee and it was typical of her commitment that she was at Burnham Market to watch me compete, making my trip there all the more worthwhile.

Now I could do as I had planned and give Stan a break for three or four weeks to freshen him up, and meanwhile continue preparing Solo for Badminton. I had horses to ride at Goring Heath, Weston Park and Bicton, but I didn't give Solo another run before Badminton, as I didn't think he needed it. We'd learnt during the Foot and Mouth outbreak, when we hadn't been able to compete, that the experienced horses seem to go just as well, if not better, when they haven't had many outings. When William Fox-Pitt's horse, Tamarillo, was off for twelve months to recover from an injury, he came back to win Badminton 2004 having competed in just one Open Intermediate event beforehand.

Unfortunately, the theory didn't quite work for me this time. While William produced a brilliant cross-country round on Tamarillo to go into the lead, I landed up diving headfirst into the Lake. It wasn't as if we weren't wet enough already: the weather was appalling and the course had become very muddy and deep. I had been drawn about fortieth, which meant that I did the steeplechase before the organisers decided to increase the optimum time on it to allow for the bad going. So I had pushed Solo to get within the original time, which in itself was quite tiring for him in those conditions.

He came off the 'chase lacking inspiration, and I was tempted to pull him out there and then. He's a much better horse on top of the ground. His second, third and fifth placings at Badminton were all on good ground, whereas at his first Badminton in 1999 the ground was wet and he didn't go very well (I fell off him twice and we were eliminated). So here we were in 2004 on wet ground again. Of course, in hindsight, I should have retired before the cross-country, but the horse is a real trier, he digs deep, and the way things were panning out I thought that if I could just coax him round I'd be well in the hunt. The horse was fourteen years old, and I had nothing to lose from trying – as long as I didn't injure him or myself.

All these thoughts were going through my head as I rode along the second phase of Roads and Tracks. I had heard quite a few results on the loudspeaker and it was obvious that people were having trouble, and that many weren't getting home. I knew Solo was capable of jumping this course, but equally that he wouldn't like the ground. "Come on, get a grip," I said to myself in the end, "Badminton only happens once a year, and there's everything to play for. If we run into trouble, I'll pull him up." So we went.

We had a good round until we got to the Lake, and at this stage we were clear and going reasonably well on the clock, so we were still competitive. There was a hedge going into the water and it was set back from the edge of the Lake just enough for there to be a patch of dry land on the far side of it. Shear H20 has never been the boldest of horses when jumping into water and, being old, experienced, and very canny, he was quick enough to spot this dry patch as he took off. His immediate reaction was to shut down behind in an attempt to get his front legs on the dry land before hitting the water, but as he dropped his back legs he caught his stifles on the brush. The effect was momentarily to stop all momentum, except mine.

I knew where I was going, I knew it wasn't the place to be doing it, and I knew I was looking very silly, but there was nothing I could do about it. To make it worse, these things always feel as if they are happening in slow motion. Basically, as the horse's back legs stalled him, his front end came down very steeply and I just slid down his neck like a child going down a slide – headfirst. The horse scrambled on over the hedge and then swam all the way to the end of the lake – he probably didn't want to carry on, so he was making damn sure he didn't. He hadn't actually fallen, and I suppose I might have just managed to stay on board if I'd been in more of a safety seat position. I'm aware that I do sometimes ride a little too forward for cross-country. Anyway, it was too late to think about what I might have done. I was drenched, the horse was drenched, and the saddle was drenched. There was nothing else for it but to make a quick exit in the direction of the stables.

I was very cross with myself but I couldn't be cross with Solo. He is my favourite. He's the first horse that I have had from the age of five and been able to keep right the way through until he reached the top of the sport. I've been lucky enough to have had some good horses come to me later in their lives, or good ones that I've started competing that have been sold on, but he's the first one that I've had ever since he was a youngster and he's done everything for me. He's not the most talented horse I've ever ridden, but he tries so hard and has such a big heart that he has more than compensated for that, and for five years he has been one of the leading horses in the world. He knows how to compete and he always rises to the challenge, as he proved so well at Burghley later in the year, when he dug very deep inside his big heart to finish a tough course in appalling conditions and take us into fifth place.

So we headed home. Next was Windsor, where I rode Arctic Fox Too in the CIO two-star event, and we finished fifth. A couple of weeks later we had two horses at Bramham, Fox on the Run and Another Garrison. I withdrew Fox on the Run after the dressage because his score wasn't very competitive and I didn't think the going on the cross-country would suit him, but Another Garrison had a good run and we finished eleventh. By now I had been told that I was definitely on the team for Athens, so Stan had come back into work and I had intended to run him at Syde Park, Tythrop Park and then Aston le Walls. But it was the middle of June and there'd been a dry spell, so the ground at Syde Park was quite hard and I decided not to do the cross-country. He'd already done a decent dressage there and was clear in the show jumping, so I was pleased about that.

I had a lot of novice and pre-novice horses competing at the time. I took three to Syde Park and seven to Salperton Park the following week, and then Trina and I managed to squeeze in a week's holiday before taking six to Shipton Moyne at the beginning of July, and three novices plus two intermediate horses to Tweseldown two days later. Taking a holiday at the end of June was one of the best things we ever did. We had been flat out working on the house all winter, so there had been no chance of a break then, and anyway we didn't have any spare money. Once the competition season had started, it was difficult to find a time when we could get away, but Jeremy had bought a flat in Marbella and offered us the use of it, so we flew out from Birmingham on the Monday after the event at Salperton Park and came back the following Sunday, only missing one weekend of competing.

I don't think either of us had realised how exhausted we were. Trina hadn't stopped working on the buildings since the beginning of November; she'd put in hours and hours, and was also helping me at the events, so she must have felt worse than me. When we got to Marbella, I spent most of the first three days asleep. We'd get up in the morning, go down to the beach, have some lunch, and then I'd go back to bed again and sleep all afternoon. Then I'd manage some supper, and by 10.30pm I'd be ready for bed again. I thought there must be something wrong with me, but after three days I felt great. The weather was fantastic, and it was just what we needed to recharge our batteries. We came home refreshed and ready to take on the remainder of what was potentially a very important year.

By the time we got back to England there had been enough rain to soften the ground slightly, so Stan was able to have his penultimate run before Athens at Tythrop Park, where we had a very satisfactory outing. He scored 26.7 in his dressage and was clear in the show jumping and the cross-country to win his Open Intermediate section. For a horse of his calibre, this wasn't a serious challenge, but that's not a bad thing in the lead-up to a championship because it gives a horse confidence. When preparing for a championship there is always the thought in the back of your mind that you need to keep the horse out of trouble, but you can't let yourself start thinking that you mustn't do things – go for a gallop or do a cross-country round – in order to keep the horse sound. If I know that I have done my best to prepare a horse and have left no stones unturned in its management and care, then if something goes wrong it's probably just bad luck. It is a tense time and I do worry to a degree, but if you worried about it all the time you'd go mad.

I was certainly very focused on the Olympics from the start of the year. We were one of the strongest teams going to the Games and, on the back of Sydney, our aim was clearly to win the team gold. But the outcome in Athens was even less predictable than usual because of the introduction of the short format (i.e. the removal of the roads and tracks and the steeplechase phases). None of us knew quite how it would pan out – whether, for example, it would work against us by reducing the influence of the cross-country, normally Britain's strongest phase. We were all very aware that our dressage and show jumping had to be of the highest possible standard so that we could be competitive in all three parts of the event. We also felt that the horses needed to be just as fit as they would have been for a normal three-day event championship with the roads and tracks and the steeplechase included. There had been talk about horses hitting brick walls (not literally) about three-quarters of the way round on the cross-country of the short format events, but we weren't sure if this was because the horses just weren't fit enough or because they hadn't been warmed up sufficiently before starting. We weren't going to be taking any chances on that, so we all got our horses as fit as usual.

There was a final team training session at Eddy Stibbe's yard about three weeks before we left for Athens. Eddy, a Dutch rider, is a fantastic host to us all and the facilities at his yard in Bedfordshire are amazing. There are about forty stables, two all-weather gallops, steeplechase fences, cross-country fences, a large indoor arena and two all-weather arenas. With such an extensive training area, the riders are always very happy to be based there, which helps to create a good atmosphere. There aren't many people who would put up with having their yard invaded by a bunch of riders, trainers, horses and grooms, and still look after us so well. He is incredibly generous to allow the British squad to take over his yard in this way, especially as he is not even British. We usually have dinner in the house at least once while we are there, and on the Press Open Day Eddy also put up a marquee on the lawn and organised lunch for everyone.

While we were at Eddy's yard we attempted to have a show jumping practice under floodlights, so that we could get a feel for what it would be like in Athens for the final (individual) show jumping round, which was scheduled for the evening. The trouble was that in July in England it doesn't get dark until about 11pm, so we felt that the best thing to do would be to go down to the pub to wait for it to get dark. We had a nice Chinese meal and a drink or two, by which time none us felt much like getting the horses out for another training session. To make things worse, it had started to tip down with rain. We did begin to wonder if it was worth the effort.

The horses must have thought we were completely mad, dragging them out their stables in the middle of night and in the pouring rain to practice show jumping, especially as they had already done some work that day. They spooked at the shadows and got drenched in the rain. Somehow it didn't seem to bear much resemblance to what we would experience in Athens, but it did at least give us an idea of what it would be like to have to come out and compete at night time, which, mentally, was a very good exercise. Normally we can put the horses away at the end of the day and forget about them for the rest of the evening, but this time, even though we'd gone to the pub, we couldn't switch off completely because we were conscious that we still had the show jumping practice to come. As for the horses, we hoped it would make it less of a surprise for them in Athens when they found themselves being taken out of their stables to jump again during the evening.

Our final event before Athens was at Aston le Walls, where Nigel Taylor had put on a special section for the short-listed horses and worked very hard to make the going on the cross-country as near-perfect as possible. He had set out the dressage in the all weather menage, and put flags all around the arena to get us in the mood for Athens. By now Stan was achieving consistently good dressage marks, and I was also pleased that we had had clear show jumping rounds at our last three events. At Aston le Walls we did the four-star dressage test, the one we would do in Athens, and Stan turned in another good performance. He did have one show jump down, and I felt that there was still a bit of room for improvement here, but Nigel had build a testing course, so I wasn't disappointed with the result. I took both horses (Solo was there as well) steadily on the cross-country. Although it's a big track and you've got to go out positively and attack it, there was no point in aiming for a fast time. The main thing was to stay focused and give Stan a good ride, because this last run was the one he would take with him in his mind to the most important competition of his life. I wanted him to be going to Athens with a smile on his face.

12
Athens

I had intended to pack in the evening before leaving for Athens, but that plan didn't quite come off because I got waylaid after dropping Trina and Stan at Kenneth's yard in the afternoon. Kenneth was going to drive them to the airport for me because Yogi didn't want any of the team riders hanging around at the airport waiting for the horses to be loaded. We had learnt from past experience that when you deliver horses for a flight the boxes aren't allowed to leave the airport until all the horses are loaded and the plane has taken off. They like you to stay there in case, for any reason, the flight doesn't go, but it can mean that you get home very late – and then, of course you have to be up early the next morning to catch your own flight.

Once I had delivered Trina and Stan, I dropped the lorry off at the garage where I had arranged to have some work done on it while we were away. I had asked Andy Potter, who lives about ten minutes from the garage, if he could pick me up and give me a lift home. Andy and his wife Lynn own a part share in a horse I ride called Another Garrison, and they very kindly offered to take me out for a meal before dropping me home. We had a great evening, but by the time they had taken me back home after a very good dinner it was probably later than it would have been if I'd gone to the airport. So the next morning I was up early, frantically throwing everything together, and making sure I was wearing the right kit – the Olympic jacket, T-shirt and trousers which had been issued to all the British athletes.

Trina's mother came to pick me up and drive me to Yogi's house, and I went with him to the airport to meet up with the rest of the team – Pippa Funnell, William Fox-Pitt, Sarah Cutteridge, Jeanette Brakewell and the reserve, Mary King. I got a text message from Trina saying that she and the horses had arrived safely, so I was beginning to feel fairly relaxed. We would have a week in Athens before the Games started with only one horse to exercise, and in fact I wasn't even going to be doing that start with, so I was in for quite an easy time.

Arriving in Athens was exciting, especially as we were staying in the Olympic village with the other athletes, rather than in a house outside the city, as we did in Sydney. The village was quite quiet to start with because a lot of the athletes hadn't arrived, but as the week went on the excitement built up and we felt very much a part of it all. The only drawback was that you never got the chance to retreat into your own space. Normally at a European Championships, or even a World Championships if it is held near enough, we take our own horseboxes, so you have your home with you. It also means that you are on site much more and there is greater flexibility about when you can ride your horse.

In Athens there was a daily schedule and each team was allocated certain times to use certain arenas. It was a forty-minute bus ride from the Olympic village to the equestrian site at Markopoulis, and we had some quite early starts, so we would ride the horses and then not have much else to do for the rest of day. The beach was quickly located, and we would spend a few hours there before coming back to ride the horses again later in the day. It was very relaxed and restful, which I think was a good thing, because often we arrive at these events already tired, having been rushing around on the circuit in England.

We were very impressed with the facilities and organisation at Markopoulis. We had gone out expecting the worst, because there had been so much bad press about the preparation for these Games. At Markopoulis, which was about forty kilometres south of Athens, everything was brand new, and there appeared to have been no expense spared. The arenas, training areas and stables were all wonderful, so there were no complaints there. The only hiccup we had was with the transport was on the morning after the opening ceremony, when the whole system was apparently still suffering from the late finish the night before. When our bus finally arrived, we all got on and promptly nodded off to sleep as usual. We awoke some time later to find the bus driving over a series of unfamiliar bumps, and when we looked out of the window we found that, after an hour's driving, the bus had gone all the way round the campus and come back to where it had started from. It had set off without a security person on board, which was obligatory for all the buses, so we'd come back to collect him, and to have the bus checked for bombs.

On the whole the security wasn't too rigid. We had the usual body and bag checks as we went in and out of the equestrian site, but nothing worse than usual, and you become oblivious to it after a while. I do remember one day, though, Yogi had a sense of humour failure because the security guards insisted on confiscating all the food we had in our bags, even our bottles of water, which seemed ridiculous. I suppose they wanted us to buy from the food stalls on the site. Anyway, Yogi got so cross about this that he decided to ignore the security guards and just walked past them without stopping. They got very worked up about that, and although they didn't go quite as far as aiming their guns at him, he was certainly forced back to the check point and relieved of his bottle of water. The only other time that the security seemed a bit extreme was when we went to a party at the British Embassy one evening. Princess Anne was there, along with a lot of other high profile people, and I did think, "If someone decides to blow this up, can we really stop him?" We were out in the garden, which was beautiful, and we had a fantastic party, but we were very conscious of the helicopters buzzing overhead and of all the security staff around the Embassy. It was a bit unnerving.

On the night of the opening ceremony we went to a party at the British Olympic Association's lodge, just outside the Village, where you could meet up with family and friends. Although Trina came along that evening, most of my other connections decided against making the journey into Athens for the night. My mother and Trina's mother had organised their own accommodation with a group of their friends, who all seemed to be having a good time. Dad wasn't there – he said he wanted to stay behind to look after his dogs – but to be honest, I think the real reason was his dislike of flying. Jeremy and Susan Lawton were out there, and also Steve Green and his wife, Sharon. The other members of Solo's syndicate, Dick Bushnell and Elf Reddihough, hadn't been able to get out to Athens.

Fortunately, Rosemary Barlow had managed, against all odds it seems, to organise another excellent base for the British horse trials supporters, and it was the ideal place to meet up with everyone. Because there is such strict access to the stables and training areas at the Olympics, your friends and family can't come to see you, so it is always great to have Rosemary's tent at these events, although after her experience in Athens, I'm not sure that she'll be keen to organise another one. For some reason known best to themselves, the Greek groundsmen at the equestrian site refused to run a television cable to the tent, so that there was no close circuit television for all the supporters on cross-country day. Organising the food was also a nightmare because the health and safety regulators threw out the original caterers after the first couple of days, so Rosemary had to send out for sandwiches. Somehow, she kept the whole thing up and running, as only Rosemary could, and we were all very glad that she did.

The BOA had recommended that athletes with competitions starting within 48 hours of the opening ceremony should not take part in the ceremony because it ended so late, so we watched it all on a big screen at the lodge. Obviously, it would it have been great to have been a part of the ceremony, as I was in Atlanta, but at three o'clock in the morning, the time I would have got back to my rooms, I might have regretted going. The next day was the first trot up, which fortunately didn't cause any anguish. The heartache for Sarah Cutteridge had come earlier in the week when she had to withdraw Wexford Lady because of a minor injury. I really felt for her. I'd been there, but even so I'm not sure that I was much help to her. When it happened to me in Atlanta, sometimes I wanted company and sometimes I didn't. Sometimes people were coming up to me to commiserate and I'd be thinking, "Please leave me alone." Other times no one would be talking to me and I'd be thinking, "I need some support!" You don't know what to feel, and it's very tough.

To make matters worse, as soon as your horse is withdrawn from the competition you are stripped of your accreditation (which is passed on to the reserve rider) and so you are no longer allowed back into the stabling area. Not only are you out of the competition but you are kicked out of your stable and accommodation, and you can't come to the event to watch everyone else unless you can get a pass or a ticket. You feel like a leper. Sarah handled it all fantastically well and was very professional, which made it easier for the rest of us, and luckily the BOA eventually managed to sort out a pass for her, so that she could come to watch the event. At the same time as feeling sorry for Sarah, we had to try to feel enthusiastic for Mary King who, having spent her first few days in Greece in a remote, rat-infested farmhouse next to where her horse was stabled, suddenly found herself at the Olympic venue getting ready to compete in the Games. It was great to have her there though, and in the end she did a brilliant job for the team.

By now Stan was working really well, largely because I hadn't been riding him! Tracie Robinson had been doing all the work for me. As the competition rules about other people riding your horse didn't come into force straight away, we had decided this would be the best policy. Tracie was more likely to work the horse in a way that he needed at that stage, whereas I would have been riding him with the competition in mind and probably asking for too much. Tracie was able to do all the loosening and supplying exercises without putting too much pressure on the horse, getting him to work correctly but in a relaxed frame of mind. I probably would have tried to skip the loosening work and gone straight on to doing some of the test movements, like shoulder-in, to reassure myself that we could still do them.

Stan had been with me for seven years, so I knew him inside out – probably too well – and sometimes in that situation tensions can build up. When Tracie had ridden him for me during our training sessions he always felt better when I got back on, and when the horse goes better, I can ride better. It has a knock-on effect. So we agreed that she should ride him in Athens to start with, which was fine by me. I was more than happy to sit back and let someone else do the work. I didn't start riding him until the Wednesday evening, four days before the competition began, when we had a practice over some jumps in the main arena under the floodlights, which was very useful. Although the stands were almost empty, it did give us a good feel of the real thing – more so than our effort in the pouring rain at Eddy Stibbe's yard anyway.

As a team, we felt pretty confident at these Games. We knew we had a strong unit of world-class riders on world-class horses and that we ought to have the edge on a lot of the other teams. Personally, I had never felt better prepared for a competition. By the time we'd got Athens, there was nothing we hadn't done – we'd put our all into getting ourselves ready. I'd started training at the beginning of the year, working on our weaknesses. I'd run the horse sparingly and been able to give him a break when I'd wanted to, and I'd forgone Badminton on him. We had focused totally on the Games, and I felt good about it. I think if you know you've done everything possible, you don't feel guilty about anything that goes wrong: it's just down to bad luck.

Although I knew I was very much a team player, I can't deny that in the back of my mind there was always the dream that if I got everything right, and some of the leading riders after the dressage made mistakes, there would be a chance of an individual medal. I woke up from my dream rather abruptly when I saw the cross-country course. It was certainly on the soft side, and for me to have any chance of a good individual place, I knew the cross-country needed to be tough, because this was my strongest phase. It was here that I was hoping to make up some ground, as I had done in Punchestown the previous year.

Our first reaction after walking the course was, "What haven't we seen? Have we missed something?" We weren't sure if we were just being a bit complacent, or if it really was as we perceived it – a three-star course with a couple of four-star fences (namely, the first water complex and the coffin). It was a bit disappointing, but we felt it shouldn't matter too much for the team because we knew that we could hold our own in the dressage and show jumping. Pippa and William were likely to produce top class dressage tests, and the rest of us should be good enough to back them up. As it turned out, we did go into the lead after the dressage, but things didn't go quite so smoothly after that.

With Tracie helping me to prepare for my dressage, everything was going well as the start of the event drew near. We were still trying to keep Stan in a relaxed state, often just hacking about or doing work in a jumping saddle to keep off his back. He is a very sensitive horse, and has quite an excitable nature, so his whole programme in the run-up to the competition was planned around keeping him relaxed and happy. Tracie and Trina had the whole thing worked out, and I just did as I was told.

Our team running order had already been agreed. Under the new rules for the short format, the teams now had five riders, which further complicated the decision-making process. Understandably, Jeanette had wanted to go first, because the only time she hadn't been the pathfinder for the team was the previous year in Punchestown, where she had a fall on the cross-country. But I didn't want to go second because I'd been second in Pau, for the European Championships, where things had gone belly up, and second again in Jerez where I made that silly mistake on the cross-country. We had all agreed that Pippa and William should go fourth and fifth, so that left third place, which in the end I was quite happy with. Initially, I had thought that going first could be my lucky spot, because I had done so well in Punchestown in that position. In fact, I did a lot of thinking about it, and eventually came to the conclusion that sometimes you can read too much into these things, thinking that you've done well just because you went in a certain position in the team. In the end I told myself just to get on with it.

Tracie helped me come to terms with my place on the team by giving me advice on how to handle it. She told me not to start watching the dressage and thinking, "Help, that was a good test. How am I going to beat that?" She said that just because someone has produced an amazing score, it doesn't mean you should start worrying about trying to do better, as it just puts more pressure on you and your horse. You've got to go out there and ride your best test and get the best mark that your horse can get.

I tried to prepare myself by thinking more about how well the horse was going and trying to fulfil my own and my horse's potential. If I didn't get anxious, then perhaps he wouldn't. Our test was quite early on the second day, so there weren't too many people watching, but it was very windy. All the flags were flapping about and the arena flowerpots kept blowing over. Shear L'Eau doesn't normally get silly and spooky on these occasions, but he can get quite tense, and then he won't release himself so his paces become a bit tight. To make matters worse, the Greek spectators were applauding every rider at the start of the test as they made their first halt and salute at X, which wasn't ideal.

As we came into the stadium and were walking around the edge of arena there was huge applause. I'm not sure if it was for the previous rider's score or because they had just announced my name, but to my surprise Stan didn't even flinch. So we started cantering, and still he remained completely focused. I was thinking, "Is this good or bad?" I would have liked him to have taken just a little bit of notice so that I could say to him, "No, come on, pay attention." But he just stayed there, down the reins, into the contact. We cantered down the centre, halted at X, and the clapping started. Again, he remained relaxed and he wasn't looking to move off. So I stayed at X a bit longer than I would normally have done and took the opportunity to breathe! I thought, "He's really focused," and it gave me huge confidence.

I was feeling good and I remembered what Tracie had said when we had been watching some dressage tests the previous day: a mistake-free test would get me the marks. It was amazing how many mistakes were being made in some very good tests. So that was what I was aiming for, and I think that apart from some slight resistance in the rein back, we achieved it. All four changes were correct – none of them were late behind and they were all on the marker. Stan kept his four loop serpentine canters and didn't change behind; he didn't jog in his walk; he was relaxed in the lateral work in the trot; he was straight and careful (perhaps a little bit too careful: he could have been slightly braver) but as we went through the test I kept thinking that it was still mistake-free. We got to the last flying change, and that was good; then it was down the centre line and I was thinking, "Crikey, we're still mistake-free, don't let him switch legs, get your balance right, get a good halt. We've done it! No mistakes!"

It was because we had a mistake-free test that we finished in tenth place at the end of the dressage on a score of 43.20. Stan is not an extravagant mover. He doesn't make people think, "Oh, wow!" when they watch him, but his outline was good and his paces were regular. They've got to give you marks for that; it's when you start making mistakes that they take the marks off. I don't think we could have produced a better test than we did. If I had asked for more, he might have made a mistake.

Pippa and William followed me with brilliant tests. Pippa scored 31.4 on Primmore's Pride to put her in second place behind France's European champion Nicolas Touzaint on Galan de Sauvagere, and with William's score of 38.60 on Tamarillo our team went into the lead. But we were only ahead of France by a fraction of a penalty, and Germany were 1.2 penalties behind us. We were all aware that the cross-country wasn't likely to change the scores much, so there was little to choose between the first three teams. Any remaining hopes that I might have had of an individual award were well and truly buried. Sometimes you can be lying tenth in an event and think, "I could win this from here if the competition goes my way," but looking at the people ahead of me in Athens, and given the relative ease of the cross-country course, there was clearly no opening. When you've got people like Pippa, William, Bettina Hoy (Germany), Kimberley Severson (US), and French riders Nicolas Touzaint and Jean Teuleure (the World Champion) in front of you, there's not much chance of gaining ground.

Our preparations for the cross-country all went smoothly. As it was everyone's first experience of the short format at a championship, we were a bit concerned about the amount of warming up that we should do to compensate for the missing roads and tracks and steeplechase. I took Stan out in the morning just to give him a quiet hack for about twenty minutes, and I then I got him out again 45 minutes before my start time, hacked to the cross-country, and trotted and cantered and jumped a few fences to warm him up. It sounds strange to say that we had to warm up in a hot climate, but you have get the horse's heart rate up and his muscles working. After I had brought him back to trot and walk, I spent about ten minutes with him in the shade under the water-mist sprays. I decided not to get off him, as he can get quite excited, so I just sat there with him under the spray. It was wonderfully refreshing. You would expect to come out soaking wet, but the water evaporates so quickly that everything stays dry.

Trina washed off his neck, greased his legs, and checked his studs, and then I came out and jumped two or three more fences. We had to be ready about four minutes before our start time because there was quite a long walk through a tunnel under the road to get from the warming up area to the start of the cross-country. Yogi walked through with me so that he could lead me into the start box.

I'd already watched Jeanette's round on the closed circuit TV monitor, so I knew that she had gone the long way between the drop fence and the obstacle with a Greek urn on top of a step, which came near the end of the course, but she had got a few time faults. The plan had been that if Jeanette could go clear inside the optimum time in spite of taking this longer option, then we would all ride that route because it was safer, but Jeanette had obviously struggled to get near the time and she is usually fast on the cross-country. Mary had gone clear inside the time taking the straight route, so Yogi and I agreed that I needed to go straight everywhere. The course seemed to be riding well and wasn't too slippery. We were lucky, too, that it was quite a breezy day and so the horses weren't getting too hot.

My main concern had been the first water complex, which consisted of a large rounded palisade fence going into the water, followed by two corners. There were three generous strides to the first corner, and then two strides to the second corner. Like his brother, Stan's first stride in water tends to be very slow. It's not a bold stride, so it is difficult for him to make the distance comfortably when there is a related distance between the fence going into the water and the next one. Kenneth Clawson and I had spent the best part of an afternoon up at the water complex trying to work out what would be the best way for me to ride this combination. In the end we agreed that I should make a bit of a dog-leg between the fence into the water and the first corner, and fit in four strides, rather than committing to three, and then ride for the two strides between the corners.

The first bit worked – I got the four strides all right and jumped the first corner – but then it went wrong. I rode for the two strides to the second corner, but we were still a long way off and Stan put down again for a third. By then we were right underneath the fence and he literally climbed over it, so it all looked a bit scary. For a split second I thought I'd had it, because when you're in that close to a fence you're on the side of a stop. But a really good event horse will do what he did – keep going and get you out of trouble. You wouldn't want to put a horse in that situation every day, but if you do make the occasional mistake a genuine horse will help you out, and Stan is 100 per cent genuine. Not only did he have the decency to climb over the fence, but he also stayed on his feet when he got to the other side.

It was a lucky escape, but I didn't let myself dwell on it. I just thought, "Okay, we got away with that and the next fence is coming up, so let's give him a good ride over that and restore confidence." After that, the course rode to plan. Stan hit a good rhythm and was jumping well. It was a great feeling. Riding the cross-country at an Olympic Games is one of the few occasions when you hear noise and applause from the crowd. The atmosphere is more intense, and people cheer as well as clap, so it can give you quite a lift. There was certainly a big cheer when I got through the first water.

As a team, we had mixed feelings about the outcome of the cross-country day. Overall, everything had gone according to plan, and all five members had come home clear, and yet we had lost ground, dropping to third place because of our time penalties. The scores had been so close that we couldn't afford these, particularly as the top teams had had no trouble in getting at least three members clear on the cross-country. It had been especially difficult for Pippa on the big-striding Primmore's Pride, a horse that really needed a galloping track as well as fences that were big enough and testing enough to back him off, neither of which he had. Pippa did a fabulous job to bring him back safely in the time that she did, but it meant that the team had 11.2 time faults of hers to add to the score and also 1.20 time penalties of mine.

I was annoyed about my time penalties. I shouldn't have let that happen. We were cruising around the course, well up on time as we approached the second water, and although the last part of the track was twisty, that wasn't really a concern for me because Stan doesn't pull, so I didn't expect to lose much time there. I think I just eased up a bit too much at about the six-minute mark, and then it took a bit longer than I expected to get through the sunken road obstacle and suddenly I was running out of time.

Nevertheless, my score still counted, together with Pippa's and William's, to take the team into third place: only six points behind Germany and 12.20 points behind France at the end of the cross-country, so we were still in touch. Everything would depend on the next day's show jumping. It wasn't until later that evening that our position took a serious turn for the worse. William's horse Tamarillo, who had gone brilliantly on the cross-country to finish within the time, had somehow chipped a bone on his stifle while out on the course, and would have to be withdrawn. This was devasting for William, who had achieved the best score on the British team at this stage and had been well placed to get an individual medal.

With William out, Mary's score now counted. It was only 9.4 penalties more than William's, but the team scores were all so close that we dropped down to fourth place below the USA and were only 0.40 points ahead of Australia, so even a team medal was now looking doubtful. A deep sense of gloom and disappointment descended on the British camp. It seemed unbelievable that we had started the day off in gold medal position. We talked it all through and, as we analysed the score, we realised that there was still a chance of a medal. We had come a long way since Sydney, when we missed winning the gold medal because our show jumping wasn't good enough. In Jerez we had managed to pull ourselves up to the bronze medal place on the final day, so there was no reason why we shouldn't do the same here. By the end of the evening we had talked ourselves out of our despondency and into a state of determination. The next day we would go out and jump for the bronze medal.

Trina had done a brilliant job in caring for Stan after the cross-country, and he came out the next morning looking and feeling very well. He wasn't tired and he wasn't sore. I'm sure that was one of the reasons why he jumped so well. I walked the show jumping course with Kenneth and then watched some of the earlier riders go, which was a bit demoralising because poles were coming down right, left and centre. These days the show jumping courses tend to be light and airy, and the cups are so shallow that you only have to touch the poles and they spring out.

My first concern was to go well for the team. Individually, I was lying eleventh at that stage, so there was little thought about my own placing even though the first show jumping round would count towards that. My warm up went well. I felt confident rather than nervous. I think it was because the preparation, with both Kenneth and William Funnell watching and helping, was good, and also because Yogi had said to me, "Go in there and jump as if you're at home." That seemed to help, though of course when we went down the tunnel and into the arena it didn't feel much like home.

But it was good advice, and that's what I tried to do. It's very easy in that situation to try to help the horse too much, which you wouldn't do at home. We got into a good rhythm and it was going well, but by the time we got to the wall, the fourth from the end, I was aware that I had gone to my hands and was overdoing it a bit. I was beginning to lift the horse over the fences with my hands, and once you start doing that it's difficult to stop. The trouble is, the more you use your hands the more chance there is of the horse dropping his back legs on the fence. I did it again at the next fence, the oxer over the water tray, but fortunately, as I turned back to the treble I found a forward distance going into it, which meant that I had to soften the arm to get there. Once I'd broken the cycle I was able to regain my composure. I knew I mustn't go to my hands again at the final fence – the planks – however big the temptation. Two years ago I'd lost my chance to win Burghley by doing that.

Stan did just rub the planks, but thankfully they stayed up. Pippa then jumped clear and our bronze medal hung in the balance as the last American rider, Kimberley Severson, went in to jump. She was clear – until the last fence – and I know what that feels like! So the bronze was ours. It was a fantastic feeling to have salvaged a medal after all the knocks we had taken.

We then had a long wait before the evening jumping, which would determine the individual medals. By now Pippa had moved up to fourth place and I was in fifth, so I suppose it did cross my mind that we could be on for an individual medal, particularly as there was some doubt about Bettina Hoy's score. We had seen her cross the start line twice in her first show jumping round, yet she hadn't been penalised, so people were beginning to talk about it. Soon afterwards, we were told that the Ground Jury (the three judges) had awarded her fourteen time penalties, which meant that the German team would drop down to fourth place and we would get the silver. But this was hadn't been confirmed on the scoreboard, so we weren't sure about it until we started walking the course for the individual show jumping. Then we saw it on the screen. Britain had got silver.

The next piece of information we received was that the Germans were appealing against the decision. I tried not to think about it. I needed to concentrate on my next round. The course was bigger, and I watched the first few competitors to see how it rode before going to the training area. When you're warming up, you don't want to get on the horse too early or too late, so you keep talking to the stewards to find out how many there are to go before you. At this point, Bettina was lying eighth, having had the fourteen penalties added to her score, so she should have gone in to jump before me. But I became aware that she hadn't even started warming up and it was nearly time for me to go in, so then I realised that the Appeals Committee must have overturned the Ground Jury's ruling and put her back into second place, which meant that Britain was back in the bronze medal position.

It would have been easy to be distracted by all the confusion and discussion that was going on about Bettina's score, but I think that's where age and experience helped me. I had a round to jump and that's what I focused on. Everyone else could worry about the rights and wrongs of the Appeal Committee's decision.

As I went into the arena I was aware that the course had been causing some trouble. I tried to imagine I was back at home, as Yogi had advised me in the first round. Again, I was trying not to try too hard. The planks were at number four this time, and we rubbed them again, giving our supporters a bit of scare because apparently the top plank swung dangerously. We came down the last line where there was a gate with a related distance to a double, then a dog-leg to the final rails, just as there had been at Burghley. To be honest, those final rails had Burghley written all over them. The temptation to try to help Stan over that last fence was enormous. There were six strides from the double down to the rails and I was talking myself through them, "Don't do it, don't do it, don't do it," and then just hoping that when I softened my hands Stan's front end would work hard enough and not knock the rail down. This time it worked. I had finally made up for Burghley, Punchestown and Pau, where my show jumping mistakes had cost me so dearly.

The feeling of achievement was incredible, and then there was the excitement of seeing all those people around you as you walk out of the arena, all with smiles on their faces, and you realise how much joy you have brought them as well. There was Trina, Yogi and Kenneth, then Jeremy appeared, and Tracie – you know that everyone is there somewhere, but you're not sure if you've seen them all. It's like a sea that comes and goes.

I was still fifth, on a score of 44.40, which was great. But looking at those ahead me – all world-class riders – I couldn't see where an individual medal could possibly come from. Next was Pippa, then the American Kimberly Severson on her brilliant horse Winsome Adante, then Bettina on Ringwood Cockatoo, and finally the European Champion Nicolas Touzaint from France, who was eleven points clear of me on a score of 33.40. None of them was likely to make a mistake.

Well, I was proved wrong. One by one they all did. Pippa had the planks down, which was bitterly disappointing for her, and then when Kimberly had a fence down, I realised I'd got the bronze medal. Bettina also had one down and collected two time penalties, but that left her on a score of 41.60, still ahead of me. Nicolas now had two fences in hand, so his claim on the individual gold medal looked like a certainty. He had already jumped a good first round, with only four faults, to help secure the team silver for France, so no one was expecting it all to go so disastrously wrong for him this time. Four fences down and three time penalties sent him plummeting down the standings. Although I felt desperately sorry for him, it did mean that I had moved up another place.

It was difficult to take in. A silver medal – where had that come from? I suddenly found myself in the middle of a whirlwind, with everyone around me going mad. It was extraordinary. I didn't think about the fact that it could have been a gold medal, had the Ground Jury's ruling on Bettina been upheld, until I was interviewed for the television by Clare Balding. She was adamant that I should have got the gold medal, so that did start me wondering whether or not the decision was right. Basically, though, I was just gobsmacked to have got the silver, and I was so delighted with the horse. He had given his best at every part of this event, right to the end: he and the American Amy Tryon's horse, Poggio, were the only two to jump double clear rounds in the show jumping. If I hadn't messed up the time on the cross-country, he would have finished on his dressage score.

There followed a slightly awkward press conference, because the journalists wanted to know what I thought about the decision on Bettina, and whether or not I was upset about it. It was difficult to know what to say, because I did think that the Appeals Committee was wrong but I didn't want to stick my neck out. Besides, I was still amazed to have got the silver. So I just said, "I don't think anyone is trying to make trouble, but rules are rules." The French were seething, understandably, because they had been told during the afternoon that they had won the gold, only to have it taken away again. So they made their feelings quite clear. There was already talk about the Americans, who finished fourth, bringing in lawyers, and possibly taking it all to the Court of Arbitration for Sport. But as far as I was concerned, it was just talk. You have to stay realistic in this sport: the ups and down are hard enough to take without getting carried away about something that may never happen.

But the next morning, I did start to hold out a bit of hope. We went to meet Simon Clegg, the Chef de Mission of Team GB, at the BOA headquarters in Athens. He began by congratulating us on what we had achieved, but then went on to say that they had been studying the whole thing during the night, and that the American, French and British lawyers were confident that we had a strong case. I did then think, "Crikey, perhaps there is a chance." They had obviously gone into the whole matter very thoroughly, and I had the feeling that they wouldn't be taking it to the Court of Arbitration for Sport unless they were pretty sure of their ground. As we left the BOA office for Athens airport to fly home, I allowed myself the thought, "Is it possible that I could really have won a gold medal?"

Epilogue

When dreams become reality, what do you do next? I know I must keep moving forward, and in any case with horses you don't have much choice. They are all out there in the yard waiting to be ridden, and needing to be prepared for their next competition. As soon as I got back from Athens, there were novice events to go to with the youngsters. There was Burghley with Shear H2O, and then there was a trip to Pau in France for the World Cup Final, where I took a talented young horse called Coup de Coeur, on whom I had just been offered the ride by Keith Scott. This ten-year-old, beautifully produced by Rebecca Gibbs, is one of best horses I have ever sat on, and so suddenly I find myself with another exciting prospect for the future and I am already looking forward to the next season.

I do think that I have been incredibly lucky to have ridden so many good horses, and to have had the breaks when I needed them. It doesn't work out so well for everyone. My younger brother, Graham, is one of the best riders I know across country, but he has found it difficult to get enough good horses to make a success of his riding career. Like the rest of my family, he works all the hours that he can, but at the end of 2003 he just wasn't making enough money to continue running his own yard and he's had to give that up.

I don't see my own story as one of rags to riches: we weren't very poor to start with and I'm certainly not rich now! As a family, we always had what we needed, even if we had to work very hard and scrape around a bit sometimes to get it. At times it has seemed like a long haul to get where I have, but I am quite a dogged, determined person and I'm happy to keep plugging away slowly to achieve what I want. Now, not only do I have an Olympic gold medal but, for the first time in my life, I also have my own house – about time, considering I am forty years old. I might even get married again. Trina and I got engaged at the end of 2000, and since then there has been a lot of banter from friends about us dragging our feet, but a wedding hasn't been at the top of our list of priorities.

Now that we have our own place, I would like to do more teaching, and perhaps have riders based here with us. When I was still at Perryfields Farm, Kylie Roddy was based with me as a student, and she got onto the Young Rider squad in 2000 and 2001, which was very rewarding. Her horse, Jennallas Boy, was just a novice when she came to us, and she took him up to three-star level, and then she sold him to the Czech rider, Jaroslav Hatla, in 2003. The horse was twelve years old then, and Kylie didn't have much money. It was a question of whether she should pin all her hopes on this one horse to get to Badminton, or whether she should sell him for a lot of money, which would then give her more options.

The sale came about because Kenneth Clawson had contacted me to ask if I knew of any horses that would suit Jaroslav, who wanted to compete in Athens. He came to see Jennallas Boy, and when he bought him he had just twelve months in which to qualify for the Olympics. He competed at Blair and Boekelo to get his three-star qualifications, and then he took the horse to Spain and Portugal and did the CICs there to gain enough points on the FEI rankings to go to Athens. So it was amazing for Kylie that within a year of selling her horse it got to the Olympics. Even better, Jaroslav went clear on the cross-country in Athens, and finished the competition in 22nd place.

It is difficult for young riders coming into the sport to find good horses and, perhaps more importantly, good owners to pay for them. Over the years I have had one or two awkward owners, but on the whole they have been fantastic, and the people that I ride for now all get on well together and have been with me for a long time. Martin Sadler, who owns Perryfields Farm, where we were based for six years, has been a very loyal owner, but he enjoys buying young horses and seeing them being made and sold on, rather than keeping them to compete at the top level. This means that I am always on the look out for young horses, and if I see something that I think is good, I just tell Martin. It's fun buying young horses, working on them, seeing them develop and seeing what happens to them once we have sold them. Martin is a very open, genuine person, and it was he who advised Trina and I to find our own place, even though we were renting his yard. "You need bricks and mortar," he used to say to us.

We also need a horsebox, which fortunately is sponsored by Jeremy Lawton, owner of the two grey brothers, Solo and Stan. Jeremy came into eventing when I began riding Solo for him, and he is now a keen follower. He set up his insurance company, Shearwater, in a room at the top of his house in Totteridge, north London, after leaving his job in the City. Initially he concentrated on horse insurance because his wife Susan was eventing at the time, but since then the company has expanded and it now covers a variety of activities. Jeremy and I have known each other for ten years, since I first started riding his horses, and have become good friends.

I also met Diana Fitzroy about ten years ago when she was a part-owner of New Flavour with Nicky Coe. I still ride Matt Butler for her, and have a nice youngster called Prairie Monarch, which is the horse featured on the poster promoting the 2012 Olympic bid in London. When they came to make the poster, they wanted to take a picture of me jumping a horse over a decent-sized fence to super-impose on a photograph of Buckingham Palace. It was November when they approached me for this, and the older horses, including Shear L'Eau, were all on holiday and had grown woolly coats. Prairie Monarch was clipped and in work – and his name was very appropriate – so we used him.

The diversity of people that I have met and become friends with through eventing has never ceased to amaze me, and it's something I hadn't expected when I started out in the sport. In my early days in Herefordshire, I never dreamt that my life would take this course and that I would cross so many different paths. I have met people from all walks of life: actors, politicians, businessmen, farmers and so on, who have all had an interest in horses, but who also have very different stories from mine, and this has added enormously to the fun of eventing. Since winning the medals in Athens, I have come into contact with even more people – most of whom don't have an interest in horses – but who have still been fascinating to meet.

The initial flurry of interviews on my return to England from Athens happened in a bit a haze. I was so exhausted after partying most of the Wednesday night after the medal ceremony, getting up early the next morning to attend the meeting with Simon Clegg at the British Olympic Association's headquarters in Athens, and then catching a flight home. I got a bit of sleep in London that night, but was up early again the next morning for interviews with GMTV and Sky, and a couple of radio stations, before heading back to Naunton to be greeted by a large gathering of people in the village. This was one of the most touching moments for me, because we had only moved into the village in February that year and had been so busy that we had hardly got to know any of our neighbours, but they turned out to welcome me home, and Trina's sister had decked our house out in Union Jack flags. There were more interviews with Central Television and BBC Midlands Today, but I eventually got away to collect Trina and Stan from Kenneth's yard where they had been waiting since their return from Athens.

When we finally got home again that evening we were shattered, but there wasn't much time to recover from it all. We had the Friday at home to unpack and sort things out before going off on Saturday morning to the Solihull horse trials, which is where Yogi contacted me to tell that I had won the gold medal. The elevation from silver to gold makes a huge difference and it had a major impact on me, one that I think will continue to influence my life and career for a long time. The initial effect was to put me in considerable demand for more interviews, to attend more functions (for example, I was awarded the BBC Midlands Sports Personality of the Year and attended the dinner for the presentation, and I was also awarded the British Equestrian Writers' Association trophy for the Equestrian Personality of the Year), to give talks to schools, to do more lecture-demonstrations, and I was even asked to do a celebrity version of The Weakest Link with the terrifying Anne Robinson. So my gold medal was already opening new doors, taking me to a lot of different places, and giving me the opportunity to meet different people.

Of all the awards and presentations, the most important to me was to receive the MBE. I was overwhelmed when I heard that I had been awarded this honour. Trina, her mother, my mother and I all went to London on February 23rd 2005, for the investiture at Buckingham Palace. It was a very special day and I felt so proud to have the MBE pinned to my jacket by the Queen. This was the icing on the cake of all that followed my Olympic gold medal win. It was a great occasion.

It was my second visit to Buckingham Palace in four months. Before the MBE ceremony, there had been the Olympic medal ceremony in London, which for me was the highlight of all the Olympic celebrations since our return from Athens. The presentations (for my gold medal, and the team silver) took place on October 18th, exactly two months after I had actually won the medal in Athens. It was the day that all the Olympic medal winners went on the open-topped bus tour of London, and it was a memorable event. I enjoyed getting back together with the rest of the team riders, and also meeting up with the other athletes and sharing memories of Athens.

The tour was great fun: lots of noise and excitement, and there was an immense crowd of people when we got to Trafalgar Square. A stage had been set up there, and the athletes were brought out onto the stage to be interviewed by Sue Barker. I can't remember exactly what she said to me, but it was something along the lines of, "Surely you were a bit annoyed and feel bitter that you didn't actually get to stand on the podium in Athens and receive the gold medal?" I said that I would be getting the medal tonight, and asked what better place there could be to receive it than Buckingham Palace. I agreed that it would have been great to have been awarded the medal on the podium in Athens, but that there was no point being bitter about it. "But what about the National Anthem? Didn't you miss that?" Sue asked. "Well, yes," I replied, "the thing that would have given me the biggest lift would have been to hear the National Anthem played on my behalf in Athens. That would have been a once in a lifetime moment." "Well," said Sue, "As you didn't get it then, we're going to play it for you today." At that point the band struck up the National Anthem and everybody started singing. It was absolutely incredible. I had no idea it was going to happen, and it was very moving.

After that we were whisked off in the bus again, with a police escort, to a hotel to change for our reception at Buckingham Palace. I knew what to expect this time, because we had been to the Palace after the Sydney Olympics, and we had a superb evening. It was all very relaxed. At the end of the reception, all the guests were ushered into the investiture room, which is like a large ballroom with seating all around the outside. Everyone was sitting down quietly – athletes, coaches and managers – when I came into the room through another door, turned right and walked up towards an area like a small stage. The Queen was there with Prince Phillip, Prince Andrew and Prince Edward. Then Princess Anne, who is a member of the International Olympic Committee, put the gold medal over my head and the place erupted with applause. It was a wonderful moment because the people who were applauding me were the other Olympic athletes. To have my achievement acknowledged by them was the most gratifying thing of all. I may not have stood on the winner's podium in Athens, but I still had my moment of glory after all.

Appendix

My Twelve Best Horses

CAPPAMORE – an Irish-bred chestnut gelding, standing at nearly seventeen hands. He was owned by Juliet Sandford, who came to work at Revel Guest's yard while I was there, and she asked me to compete him because he had grown too big for her. He usually managed to impress the dressage judges, but he was a bit flat in his jumping which meant that he didn't have quite enough scope for the higher levels. But he always tried hard, and at his own level he was difficult to beat. We won the Windsor three-day event (two-star) in 1990 and the Intermediate Championships at Locko Park. I rode him for about four years and had a lot of fun with him, and he was an important horse to me because he kept me in the picture by winning good classes at a time when I was trying to make my way in the sport.

WELTON APOLLO – a sixteen hands stallion, one of many good horses bred by Sam Barr at the Welton Stud. He was by Welton Gameful, the stallion who started the Welton dynasty and whose progeny included Welton Crackerjack (ridden by Tiny Clapham) and Welton Louis (Pammy Hutton). Welton Apollo did very well to compete regularly at four-star level as well as taking on his stud duties, and he sired some useful Junior and Young Rider horses. He played a very important part in my career because he was the first horse that I rode at four-star level, and I completed my first Badminton on him in 1987. He was the sort of horse that you had to ride positively, otherwise you risked having a stop, but he was a brilliant technician and always picked up well in front, which gave me a lot of confidence. For a stallion, he had a very laid back nature: you could put him on the lorry next to a mare to travel to an event and there would never be any fuss, so he was very easy to look after.

HAIG – a seventeen hands home-bred horse owned by Mary Archdale. He came to me after Jane Holderness-Roddam had seen him at a clinic that she had been taking. Mary was riding him at the time, but she found him a bit too big. He was a lovely, free-moving horse with enough scope to jump a house, but he was also an incredibly gentle horse, and an absolute joy to have on the yard. I won Windsor on him in 1990 (the same year that I won another section on Cappamore) and he was eighth at Bramham in 1993. He was one of only two horses that came with me to Sam Barr's yard when I stopped working for Revel Guest, but he had a leg injury soon after we moved and had to have the 1991 season off work. I had always intended to run him at Badminton – he certainly had the scope to do it – but he never quite made it. I think he was his own worst enemy in a way, because he was such a big horse and had such a big jump that he put too much pressure on his front legs.

CAPITANO – quite a small horse, only about sixteen hands, but he had the gallop of a 16.2 hands horse. He must have been thorough-bred, or very nearly, and he was like a rubber ball to ride. His power and athleticism made him one of the most exciting horses that I have ever ridden across country. Although he had the paces for dressage, his bubbly, extrovert character often got the better of me in this phase. We were tenth at Burghley in 1995 and sixteenth at Badminton in 1997 when we won the Glentrool Trophy. Elf Reddihough, his owner and breeder, had asked me to take over the ride on him when his former jockey, Danny Wilson, went back home to Australia, so he was already at four-star level when I began riding him. He was a wonderful little horse, and I was devastated when he collapsed and died of an aneurism while competing in the cross-country at the Open Championships at Gatcombe in 1997.

NEW FLAVOUR – an Irish-bred, 16.1 hands, seven-eighths thoroughbred owned by Nicky Coe and Diana Fitzroy. Nicky had produced him beautifully, and I was lucky to get the ride on him when Nicky had a baby. He was a fabulous horse: the first four-star horse I'd had that was seriously competitive in all three phases, and he came to me at a time when I was badly in need of good quality horses to ride. We were fourth at Badminton in 1996, and were selected for the Atlanta Olympics, but New Flavour was withdrawn from the team on the day of the first horse inspection because of a bruised sole. He could be quite a grumpy horse in the stable, and you had to watch he didn't bite you. The most dangerous manoeuvre when he was around was to walk down inside the lorry to check the horses on a journey. As you ducked to go under his head, you were likely to get a chunk taken out of your back. I suppose he was quite an arrogant horse, but he was joy to ride, an easy galloper and a very careful jumper. I always felt that it was such a pity he didn't get the chance to compete in Atlanta, because he was so "on song" that year. He'd been going absolutely brilliantly. There are times in a horse's career when you sense that they are at their peak, and 1996 was the time for New Flavour.

CRUISEWAY – a beautiful-looking, seventeen hands, dark brown gelding by Cruise Missile, a very good stallion stood at stud by David Eckley at the Vow Church Court Stud. I knew David and Sylvia Eckley from my Herefordshire days, and had ridden a point-to-pointer for them when I was younger. Cruise Missile had been trained for racing by Nicky Henderson and ridden by John Francombe, and he produced some very good-looking horses of which I evented quite a few, some of them for David and Sylvia. Cruiseway was owned and bred by Alan Spiers, and he'd been successfully shown in hand as a three-year-old. He had good paces and was a good jumper, but he was quite a tricky character. You certainly had to ask him to do things, not tell him! There was always a degree of compromise, because if he didn't want to do something he wouldn't do it. He had a complex personality, but we pulled off some good results: he was third at Bramham in 1996 and tenth at Blenheim the following year.

PERRYFIELDS GEORGE – a full thoroughbred, 16.3 hands, bred by Mike Cresswell, a friend of Martin Sadler who owned the horse. A gorgeous-looking chestnut horse that Martin had initially thought might make a show hunter until Robert Oliver advised him to try eventing. That was how I got involved, and I took him on as a four-year-old. He was a lovely, kind horse with good paces. I did the Burghley Young Event Horse classes with him, and he was third at the Blair Castle two-star event as a seven-year-old. He then did Bramham (where he finished seventh) and Blenheim (where he was fourth), the following year. There's no knowing where I could have gone with him – he definitely had four-star potential – but he was sold to an Italian as an eight-year-old. Saying goodbye to him was devastating for me, because he was the first horse I had produced myself from the start, and I knew he had the ability to go on. I think he was quite successful in Junior and Young Riders in Italy, but he never did a four-star event.

BRER RABBIT – a thoroughbred 16.2 hands chestnut gelding by Crested Lark out of Sun Trip. He was owned by John Bennett and had been produced to four-star level by Owen Moore. He was one of the most inspiring horses across country that I have ridden, and I had two super Badminton rounds on him. It was a pity that he had such bad front feet. They were typical thoroughbred feet: very flat and easily bruised, which meant that we had to limit how much work we did with him. We managed to get him fit enough by swimming him, but I would have liked to have been able to do more training with him on the flat to improve his dressage. He was a lovely, kind horse, and he went on to give Chris King his first ride around Badminton before retiring at the end of 2004.

MATT BUTLER – a 16.3 hands bay gelding by the Irish sire Rhett Butler, and probably about seven-eighths thoroughbred. He is owned by Diana Fitzroy and came to me as a six-year-old. A lovely horse to compete and have around, but he just didn't quite manage four-star level. He's got a big jump, so I don't think it is scope that he is short of, but perhaps endurance. It's hard to know, but he just wasn't happy on the four-star tracks. I've had some great events on him, though, particularly at Chatsworth in 2003 when he came fifth in the World Cup qualifier, and he's won some good advanced classes.

ANOTHER GARRISON – a thoroughbred sixteen hands gelding by Mandalus out of a half sister to Garrison Savannah, bought by Diana Dickinson and Lynn Potter to race. He did some point-to-points, but didn't make a successful racehorse and was sent to me as a five-year-old. He's only a little horse, but he's such an easy galloper and a very good jumper. He's had some good results, coming second in the Weston Park two-star event in 2002 as an eight-year-old, and eleventh at Bramham in 2004.

SHEAR H2O (SOLO) – a 16.1 hands, seventh-eighths thorough-bred, Irish-bred gelding by Stan the Man out of a Carnival Night mare called Starry Knight. I bought him as a five-year-old from Roland Fernyhough on behalf of Jeremy Lawton, his owner. At the time I was slightly concerned that he might be a bit too much on the chunky side, and not thoroughbred enough for the job, but I loved everything else about him. He is my favourite horse of all time. He's the first horse that I've had right from the beginning, and taken to the top of the sport, and he has put up with all my mistakes. He has taken a few knocks because of them, but he has always bounced back, which makes him an absolute dream horse. He has taught me a huge amount and even now I am still learning on him. He's been a tremendously consistent, competitive horse who always pulls his weight and is very tough: he has completed Badminton three times (finishing second, third and fifth), Burghley twice (fifth and eleventh), and has been on three championship teams (Olympics, World and European). He's the Roy Keane of the team: he has a fighter-terrier character and you can imagine him giving the other horses on the lorry a talking-to if they haven't been up to scratch. He gets very worked up at competitions, particularly when you are getting him ready on the lorry, just as Roy Keane might do in the tunnel before a big football match.

SHEAR L'EAU (STAN) – a full brother to Shear H2O, but a bigger horse, at 16.3 hands, and slightly finer. He is owned by Jeremy Lawton and a syndicate made up of Dick Bushnell, Steve Green and Elf Reddihough. Stan was initially produced in Ireland by Anne Hatton, who did a bit of show jumping with him. Roddy Dean spotted him competing, and we bought him as a five-year-old. He's sharper than his brother, very switched on, and he doesn't miss a thing. It only takes someone to pop his head round a corner or drop a pole for him to spin round and see what's going on. He's very sensitive to noise, which is why we put the ear covers on him for the show jumping in Athens, to deaden the sound slightly. He has a lovely nature, though he is a little bit shy in the stable, yet he loses that shyness when he comes out, and can be quite naughty. I think he's still improving in his dressage, and there is more to come. Like his brother, he is a good jumper and very accurate on a line – a very honest horse – and he doesn't pull on the cross-country so you can just keep riding him forward. He has taken longer to produce than Solo because of his sensitive nature, but now that he has got there he has a bit more ability. It's fortunate that, until recently, he was able to take a back seat while his older brother did the big events, which meant that we could bring him on slowly. There was no pressure on him, and I think that suited him. In 2003 and 2004 he proved he was ready for the big time.

Index